*The*

# DICTIONARY

*of the*

# UNITED STATES GOVERNMENT

# The DICTIONARY of the UNITED STATES GOVERNMENT

## 350 TERMS AND PHRASES THAT *Define Our Democracy*

EMILY LEWELLEN

ADAMS MEDIA

New York  Amsterdam/Antwerp  London  Toronto  Sydney/Melbourne  New Delhi

Adams Media
An Imprint of Simon & Schuster, LLC
100 Technology Center Drive
Stoughton, MA 02072




Interior design by Maya Caspi
Interior images © Adobe Stock


Manufactured in the United States of America

1 2026

Library of Congress Cataloging-in-Publication Data has been applied for.

ISBN 978-1-5072-2648-3
ISBN 978-1-5072-2649-0 (ebook)

Let's stay in touch! Scan here to get book recommendations, exclusive offers, and more delivered to your inbox.

# **Contents**

# Introduction

The United States government contains many moving parts, types of politicians, regional and global influences, and differing opinions. This thoughtful and complex political structure was created to represent the people living in the US and protect the rights of American citizens. To appreciate, sustain, and benefit from this nuanced government, it's important to understand its many layers and the language that surrounds it—and sometimes what you need most is to have the terms explained clearly.

In *The Dictionary of the United States Government*, you'll find 350 terms that will make understanding the most integral parts of the US political system easy. Whether you've been following US politics for years or are preparing to vote in your first election, you'll be able to understand the many varying roles in the American government and their background through this glossary of simple, accessible terms. First, each term is quickly summarized. Then, the "What it is" section provides a clear definition. Next, the "How it works" section further contextualizes and explains the concept. Finally, the "How it is used" example uses the term in an everyday sentence.

Throughout the book, you'll find the terms grouped into common categories that will help you understand each term in context. For example:

- **Chapter 1: Basics of Government** highlights words associated with government systems as a whole, not just the American government.
- **Chapter 4: The Executive Branch** explores the powers, duties, and roles of the president and the bureaucracy that execute national law.
- **Chapter 6: Political Participation** focuses on the ways people can participate in politics, exploring terms such as *electioneering, political party,* and *Voting Rights Act*.
- And more!

Ultimately, the terms found throughout *The Dictionary of the United States Government* will teach you how the American government works, the role each citizen plays in the system, and the protections guaranteed to them, in an effort to help you become more informed. Let's take a look at the language that makes the US government run, so you can understand it easily and successfully.

# Chapter 1

# BASICS OF GOVERNMENT

The idea of centralized government spans the entire world. All nations have a political system that exerts its power over people, and different governments have particular ways of organizing their power. Although this book focuses specifically on the US government, there are certain terms and ideas related to government concepts as a whole that you should know. This chapter covers those for you.

Although some of the terms discussed in this chapter might not relate to aspects of the American government, they can help you understand other political systems around the world. For example, you'll find terms about different types of government systems and key philosophies that are central to the purpose of government.

# administration



**What it is:** the act of implementing laws and programs within a government system

**How it works:** In every government system, groups approve public policies which go into effect, thereby affecting the nation's citizens. This process is called administration. Administration encompasses the execution, management, and organization of policies and programs passed by a government. In the US, the administration of policy varies depending on the political party in power. Often, political scientists and historians label a president's term as their administration—for example, the Obama administration. This gives insight into the execution of laws and programs during a president's time in office, often related to their political party.

**How it is used:** During the Bush **administration**, the government executed a war on terror as a response to the attacks on September 11, 2001.

# anarchy



**What it is:** a form of society where centralized government doesn't exist

**How it works:** Anarchy is a form of society with no rules and no laws. Typically, anarchy doesn't last for long periods of time, and it may happen when a country is between government systems. For example, if a country has recently experienced a civil war or a revolution, anarchy may persist while the country works on becoming stable again. Anarchy can translate to chaos and disorder, as there's no ruler or government system. This lack of central political framework can also describe the belief of self-governance, where people coexist and cooperate voluntarily without a formal government structure.

**How it is used:** After the collapse of the French monarchy during the French Revolution, a state of **anarchy** existed, which was marked by violence and chaos.

# authoritarianism



**What it is:** a government system where the rulers have ultimate authority (control) in most aspects of society

**How it works:** Authoritarianism describes when the central, or national, government is powerful and dominates society. Authoritarian governments demand political obedience and submission from their citizens to the authority of the rulers. Oftentimes, peoples' political freedoms are severely limited, but social organizations might still exist. Authoritarian governments can include dictatorships and monarchies, as well as countries where small groups rule. Unlike a democracy, the power of the government resides in the ruler themselves, not in the people.

**How it is used: <u>Authoritarianism</u>** existed in Nazi Germany under Adolf Hitler, as this government had extensive power over its people and their lives.

# authority



**What it is:** a political leader's right to exercise their power

**How it works:** When leaders are selected to rule a country, they've been granted the right to use the power of the government. Authority is essentially the permission they have to use power to accomplish their duties. This power can be granted through customs, laws, or elections. When people accept a political leader's authority to use power as valid, it's seen as legitimate authority. Power in a government is stable only when it comes from legitimate authority. When people don't accept the authority of a leader, it creates tension within the country.

**How it is used:** The president of the United States can use their **<u>authority</u>** as commander in chief to deploy the military during national crises.

# autocracy



**What it is:** a form of government where one person holds the power

**How it works:** An autocracy exists when only one person holds the power in a government system. This can take many forms, including a dictatorship or monarchy. Dictators are rulers who use force or intimidation to gain their power. They maintain this power as long as they're not challenged. Monarchs get their power through inheritance, passing their power to their descendants. Absolute monarchs are true autocratic governments, as the king or queen has absolute (or total) power over all things. A constitutional monarchy differs because it places limits on the king or queen through a constitution.

**How it is used:** Current forms of **autocracy** in the world include dictatorships, such as North Korea; absolute monarchies, like Saudi Arabia; and single-party nations, such as China.

# civics



**What it is:** the study and practice of being a citizen

**How it works:** Civics education is an important part of being an active citizen of a country. Learning civics includes gaining an understanding of how the government works and what your role is in that government. Civics also includes learning about the ways to participate in politics, such as through voting, joining political parties and interest groups, protesting peacefully, and petitioning government officials. Having high-quality civics education increases citizens' engagement with their government and helps to protect democracy.

**How it is used:** **Civics** is an important part of the American education system and is a required course in many states and schools.

# confederation

*power to the states*

**What it is:** a system of government where states hold the authority

**How it works:** In a confederation, the state or local governments have more power than the national government. The national government's power is severely limited. States are independent and loosely allied with each other through the national government. States retain the right to make their own laws and decisions, but they come together over interests that affect them all, such as defense and trade. The first official government of the United States was a confederation, under the Articles of Confederation.

**How it is used:** The Confederate States of America, during the American Civil War, was a short-lived **confederation** of eleven Southern states.

# consent of the governed

*permission to have power*

**What it is:** power is given to the government by the people

**How it works:** The consent of the governed is an important political concept that the founding leaders of the United States believed in. It's also a fundamental part of democracy. The idea behind this concept is that governments exist only when the people allow them to exist. People give their consent to allow the government to have power and to use that power in regard to the people themselves, which gives legitimacy to the government. Consent of the governed goes hand in hand with the idea of popular sovereignty and the social contract.

**How it is used:** The Declaration of Independence lays the foundation for the American government when it states that governments are formed by and with the **consent of the governed**.

# constitution

*government outline*

**What it is:** a plan for how the government will operate and what its structure will be

**How it works:** Every government system needs to have a plan. How the government is laid out, what it can and can't do, and how it functions are all things that can be found in any nation's constitution. By having the rules and procedures for a government written down in a constitution, there are certain limits placed on the government itself, and the country's people can refer to the constitution to determine whether a government is acting appropriately. In the United States, the country's constitution is called the Constitution, implying it's the only one. But most, if not all, countries have constitutions.

**How it is used:** The United States **Constitution** was established in 1787 and is centered around the principles of checks and balances, federalism, limited government, popular sovereignty, and separation of powers.

# democracy

*the people rule*

**What it is:** a form of government where the power resides with the people

**How it works:** Democracy was first founded in ancient Greece, where they had the idea to put the power of the government in the hands of the people. This was known as direct democracy, where the people vote on all issues. Representative democracy formed over time as nations became too large to have people vote on every issue. In this type of democracy, individuals elect representatives to make legislation and run the government. The people still have the power, as they choose the representatives. Today, the general public uses the term *representative democracy* interchangeably with *republic*.

**How it is used:** There are over one hundred countries in the world that have governments that are **democratic** in nature.

# divided government



**What it is:** when different political parties have control in different branches of government

**How it works:** A divided government occurs when the elected president is of a different political party than the majority of at least one house of Congress. Those who created the Constitution wanted the government to be slow and deliberate. A divided government slows the government down, as only public policy that's important to both parties will be created. In this way, it serves as a form of checks and balances. But when the majority of both houses of Congress and the president are of the same political affiliation, it's called a unified government.

**How it is used:** The United States experienced a **divided government** during all of President Richard Nixon's time in office, as the majority of both houses of Congress were Democrats and Nixon was a Republican.

# federal system of government



**What it is:** a system of government where state governments and the national government have separate powers but share authority over the same people

**How it works:** This system happens when power is divided between the states and national government. The US has a federal system of government, so the national government has supreme authority within its constitutional powers; states have powers of their own; and some powers—such as levying taxes—are shared between both levels of government. The founding leaders of the US settled on this system after living through both unitary and confederate systems and wanting to avoid the weaknesses of either system.

**How it is used:** During the COVID-19 pandemic, the **federal system of government** allowed for both the state and federal governments to make decisions about relief programs, vaccines, mask mandates, and lockdown procedures.

# government



**What it is:** the body of people or groups that govern a nation or country

**How it works:** Governments operate to solve problems for the nation they serve by making public policy (official laws or programs). Laws are established to preserve order and protect the rights of the people in a society. Public goods—things paid for by taxes and enjoyed by everyone, such as a public library or park—are examples of government-implemented programs. Entitlement programs are another form of public policy. These programs are also paid for by taxes but are available only for members of certain groups. Some examples of entitlement programs are Social Security, benefits for veterans, and welfare programs.

**How it is used:** The **government** created a new program that will provide aid to those who have suffered from natural disasters, such as floods, hurricanes, and tornadoes.

# inherent powers



**What it is:** the powers that a government has simply by existing

**How it works:** Some of the federal government's powers are listed in the Constitution (expressed powers), and some powers are implied (inherent powers). Inherent powers, which exist because the government exists, are necessary for the government to function and operate. For example, a government has the inherent power to enact diplomacy with other nations, regulate immigration within its borders, and acquire new land for territorial expansion. These powers are the natural domain of a government system.

**How it is used:** An example of **inherent powers** in action is the purchase of the Louisiana Territory by Thomas Jefferson in 1803.

# natural rights



**What it is:** rights that can't be taken away without reason

**How it works:** British philosopher John Locke first developed his natural rights philosophy in the 1600s. He argued that all people are created equal and have natural rights that cannot be taken away from them by the government without just cause. He stated that natural rights consisted of life, liberty, and property. Thomas Jefferson was heavily influenced by Locke when writing the Declaration of Independence but changed the term *natural rights* to *unalienable rights*—the unalienable rights of life, liberty, and the pursuit of happiness. Jefferson and the other founding leaders of the United States believed that the government's purpose was to protect the natural rights of its people.

**How it is used:** A government can't take away a person's **natural rights** without justifiable reason (like breaking the law).

# oligarchy



**What it is:** a form of government where power is held by a small group of people who take charge of the country

**How it works:** Oligarchies exist when the power and authority of a government lie within a small group. There are different types of oligarchies, determined by who is in power. If an organization of wealthy people uses its status to gain control of the government, it's considered an aristocracy. If the group in power consists of high-ranking members of the military, it's a military junta. If religious leaders are in control, it's a theocracy. Oligarchies can exist alongside other forms of government. For example, some countries might have a dictator who's financially supported by an oligarchy.

**How it is used:** Russia had an **oligarchy** in the 1990s, with leaders being heavily influenced by small groups of individuals.

# parliamentary system



**What it is:** a system of government where the powers of the legislative and executive branches aren't fully separate

**How it works:** In a parliamentary system, the legislative body elects the leader of the executive branch, often called a prime minister. As such, the prime minister will always be of the same political party as the majority of parliament. This means there's no real separation of powers and divided government (when the leader is of a different political party) will not happen. In the United States, there's a presidential system of government, where the people elect members of the legislative branch, or Congress, and indirectly elect the president. A clear separation of powers exists between the two branches. Even though the people don't elect their executive in a parliamentary system, it is still considered a democratic system of government, as the people elect members of their legislature.

**How it is used:** The United Kingdom uses a **parliamentary system** of government where Parliament elects the prime minister.

# politics



**What it is:** the decision-making process of government officials

**How it works:** When considering the government as a whole, it's important to understand politics. The concept of government dictates what the government can and cannot do. Politics is about how the government makes things happen. The study of politics includes understanding the decision-making process that members of the government go through. This includes understanding the influences that those in power experience when making decisions about policy. These influences can come from a variety of places, including political parties, the media, special interest groups, campaign donors, and ordinary citizens.

**How it is used:** Many people have negative feelings about **politics**, but it is seen as a necessary tool to get things done in any government system.

# republic



**What it is:** a form of government where individuals vote for representatives to operate the government

**How it works:** One of the first known republics was in ancient Rome, but today, a large number of countries consider themselves to be republics. In this type of government, the people elect representatives who will vote on major issues to serve as the rulers of the country. The people hold the power in a republic, as they choose their leaders and representatives. When people reference a republican form of government, they're likely not talking about the Republican Party. To differentiate between these two, people will capitalize the political party name.

**How it is used:** When asked what type of government was decided upon after the Constitutional Convention in 1787, Benjamin Franklin said, "A **republic**, if you can keep it."

# social contract



**What it is:** people give power to the government in exchange for protection

**How it works:** Philosophers developed the social contract theory during the Enlightenment period. This theory states that people agree to give up some freedoms in exchange for the government's protection of their natural rights. The government exists because the people allow it to exist. If the government violates the social contract, the people must change that government. This theory was the justification of the colonists' breaking with Great Britain during the American Revolution and is reflected in the Declaration of Independence.

**How it is used:** In the Declaration of Independence, Thomas Jefferson wrote that the thirteen colonies were justified in their independence because Great Britain violated the **social contract**.

# sovereignty



**What it is:** a country's power to rule itself

**How it works:** Sovereignty is an important component of a country, as it allows the country to rule itself without control from another nation. Before the American Revolution, the thirteen colonies didn't have sovereignty because they had to default to the ruling country of Great Britain. When the United States became independent, it gained sovereignty. Similarly, in the US today, individual states don't have sovereignty. Although states have separate governments and can enact their own laws, those laws can't conflict with the Constitution or valid federal law. In the US, this gives the national government sovereignty but not the states.

**How it is used:** There are over 197 countries that claim to have **sovereignty**, although some nations dispute this number.

# unitary system



**What it is:** a government system where the central, or national, government has significantly more power than the states

**How it works:** Under a unitary system of government, the national government holds all the real power. State, local, or regional governments might exist, but they carry out the laws and policies of the national government. The independent powers of local governments are severely limited, if nonexistent, and they rely almost entirely upon the national government. Although the United States doesn't have this system of government, many countries around the world do.

**How it is used:** The United Kingdom is an example of a country with a **unitary system** of government.

# Chapter 2

# FOUNDATIONS OF AMERICAN GOVERNMENT AND THE CONSTITUTION

To understand the American government system, you must first understand why the Constitution was created. Why did the founding leaders decide that a republic was the best government for the new United States? Why were certain concepts included, and what do they mean? The founding leaders weren't perfect, but they created a government that put together philosophical concepts in a new way, embarking on the great American experiment. Understanding their intentions with the government helps us understand what the function of government should be. Without this knowledge, you can't truly appreciate or understand how the US government has evolved over time.

This chapter provides historical context, detailing the government before the Constitution, the compromises made at the Constitutional Convention, and the resulting government that's still used today. The terms in this chapter explore the major concepts that lay the foundation for the American government system and explain why they're still important.

# 3/5ths Compromise



**What it is:** a compromise at the Constitutional Convention regarding slavery

**How it works:** At the Constitutional Convention, the issue of slavery was a source of serious debate and conflict. Northern states believed that enslaved people should be counted as part of the population for taxation purposes but not for representation in the House of Representatives, as it would give the Southern states an unfair advantage. Southern states believed the opposite — that enslaved people should count toward representation but not taxation. The compromise was that three out of every five enslaved people would be counted toward a state's population for both taxation and representation purposes. This clause was abolished with the 13th Amendment.

**How it is used:** The **3/5ths Compromise** was one of many compromises regarding slavery made at the Constitutional Convention in 1787 to keep the Southern states from leaving the convention.

# 10th Amendment



**What it is:** the amendment that grants the states powers not listed in the Constitution

**How it works:** Like the federal government, which has implied powers not listed in the Constitution, the state governments also have powers not detailed in the Constitution called reserved powers, which are granted to the states through the 10th Amendment. The last amendment in the Bill of Rights, the 10th Amendment, gives states any powers that aren't granted to the federal government or denied to the states in the Constitution. This amendment helps to establish the principle of federalism.

**How it is used:** The **10th Amendment** gives the states powers such as conducting elections, establishing education standards, and determining qualifications of voters.

# amendment process



**What it is:** the process by which changes can be made to the Constitution

**How it works:** When creating the Constitution, the founding leaders wanted to ensure that there was a way to make changes to the Constitution over time. But they didn't want this process to be easy because they wanted any changes to be important and impactful. The amendment process can be found in article 5 of the Constitution. Two-thirds of Congress, or a national convention, must approve a proposed amendment. Three-quarters of the states, whether through state legislature or convention, must also approve the amendment. This process takes time and is deliberate, just as intended.

**How it is used:** To date, there have been only twenty-seven amendments that have successfully made it through the **amendment process**.

# Anti-Federalists



**What it is:** a group of people who didn't approve of the Constitution

**How it works:** After the Constitutional Convention ended on September 17, 1787, the newly formed government was pushed out to the states to ratify the Constitution. The Anti-Federalists then emerged, believing people should vote against this new government. They wrote multiple papers trying to convince the people of the downfalls of the Constitution. Anti-Federalists said that the Constitution empowered the federal government too much because of its Necessary and Proper Clause and the Supremacy Clause. They also believed that the lack of a Bill of Rights would allow the federal government to trample on the rights of its citizens.

**How it is used:** Ultimately, the **Anti-Federalists** compromised with the Federalists and agreed to vote for the new Constitution if a Bill of Rights was immediately added.

# Articles of Confederation



**What it is:** the first government system of the newly formed United States during and directly after the American Revolution

**How it works:** When the thirteen colonies declared independence, they needed a new government system. Fearing a strong federal government after their experience with Great Britain, they developed the Articles of Confederation. Under this system, the states held the power, and the federal government was incredibly weak. In order to pass a law, nine out of thirteen states had to agree to it, and there was no way to enforce it. The national government had limited power and couldn't tax the people. This limited the government's ability to pay debts, leading to a depression and making it difficult for the federal government to fix issues.

**How it is used:** The issues with the **Articles of Confederation** ultimately led to the Constitutional Convention in 1787, where the Constitution was created.

# bicameral legislature



**What it is:** a type of legislative body that has two houses (or chambers)

**How it works:** Under the Articles of Confederation, the legislative branch was unicameral, meaning it had only one house. Those who created the Constitution decided that the government in the United States under the Constitution would be bicameral, with two houses: the House of Representatives and the Senate. Having two houses would allow for an internal check on the power of Congress, as both houses have to agree to bills before they can become law. To learn about these houses and their powers, see Chapter 3.

**How it is used:** The federal government and many states have a **bicameral legislature**, allowing for greater access to the government by the people.

# checks and balances

*limitations on each branch of government*

**What it is:** the ability of each branch of government to stop other branches from becoming too powerful

**How it works:** The concept of checks and balances allows each branch of government to regulate the power of another. This helps to stabilize the power of the government by ensuring that no one branch becomes too powerful. Examples of checks and balances include the president's ability to veto laws that Congress is trying to pass and, subsequently, Congress's ability to override the president's veto. Another example is the Senate's power of advice and consent when it comes to presidential appointments. Additionally, the Supreme Court's power to interpret laws and executive actions as unconstitutional is a major check on the power of the other branches.

**How it is used: Checks and balances** is a government philosophy developed by Montesquieu, a French judge and political philosopher.

# Commerce Clause

*regulation of trade*

**What it is:** Congress's power to regulate interstate and foreign commerce

**How it works:** In article 1, section 8 of the Constitution, the Commerce Clause gives Congress the power to regulate business and trade between the states and foreign countries. This means Congress has the power to create laws that manage how goods and services cross state lines. Congress, however, can't regulate intrastate trade (trade within a state). This power is seemingly simple in nature but has been interpreted in a variety of ways over time. It has been used to try and limit child labor as well as segregation throughout history.

**How it is used:** The **Commerce Clause** was used to help uphold the Civil Rights Act of 1964 when it was argued that segregation and discrimination in public areas had a negative effect on the commerce and economy of the United States.

# concurrent powers



**What it is:** powers that are given to federal and state levels of government

**How it works:** In the US, the federal and state governments have separate powers but do share some; these are called concurrent powers. Concurrent powers include making and enforcing laws, levying taxes, establishing courts, borrowing money, and protecting the health and safety of citizens. Concurrent powers can allow for the two levels of government to work together, or it can create conflict when both try to tackle issues.

**How it is used:** The COVID-19 pandemic highlighted the complications of **concurrent powers**, as both national and state governments tried to protect public health, at times opposing or cooperating with each other.

# Connecticut Compromise

*Great Compromise of the Constitutional Convention*

**What it is:** a compromise at the Constitutional Convention that established the structure of the United States government

**How it works:** During the Constitutional Convention, there were many debates about how the new government under the Constitution should be structured. The Connecticut Compromise, proposed by Roger Sherman and Oliver Ellsworth, took into consideration the concerns of the larger and smaller states. This compromise made the legislative branch bicameral: The House of Representatives has representation based on population, satisfying larger states. The Senate is based on equal representation, making smaller states feel represented. There are other components to this compromise, but the structure of Congress is the most influential one.

**How it is used:** Prior to the adoption of the **Connecticut Compromise**, the delegates to the Constitutional Convention debated over representation in the new Congress for close to two months.

# Constitutional Convention



**What it is:** a meeting in 1787 to create a new US government

**How it works:** The Constitutional Convention met between May and September 1787 in Philadelphia. There were fifty-five delegates from the original thirteen states who attended the convention in an effort to change the government from the Articles of Confederation, which was failing to uphold the rights of the people. They debated and compromised until finally, on September 17, 1787, they agreed on the Constitution and sent it to the states for ratification (acceptance). James Madison, who took meticulous notes throughout the convention, is the reason the public knows about what was discussed, as his notes were published after his death.

**How it is used:** The **Constitutional Convention** was attended by delegates such as Alexander Hamilton, George Washington, and George Mason.

# cooperative federalism



**What it is:** when the state and national governments work together on issues

**How it works:** Also known as fiscal federalism, cooperative federalism is when the state and national governments come together to solve problems. Like a marble cake, the two levels of government are intertwined. In these circumstances, they'll share power and funding. Oftentimes, the national government will give money to the states after issuing a federal mandate (when the national government orders the states to implement a certain policy). Cooperative federalism most often occurs during times of national crisis.

**How it is used:** Examples of **cooperative federalism** include the government issuing funded mandates during the New Deal programs and reforms and the involvement of the Centers for Disease Control and Prevention during the COVID-19 pandemic.

# Declaration of Independence



**What it is:** the document where the United States declared it was no longer politically tied to Great Britain

**How it works:** The Declaration of Independence was written in 1776 during the American Revolution. In this document, Thomas Jefferson states the purpose of government is to protect the people's natural rights. If a government can't do that, the people must then change that government. To provide justification for declaring independence, Jefferson outlined twenty-seven grievances, or complaints, the American people had regarding how the king of England treated them. Finally, he declared that the thirteen colonies were no longer politically tied to Great Britain and were independent. This document was formally accepted by the Second Continental Congress on July 4, 1776.

**How it is used:** The **Declaration of Independence** was signed by a total of fifty-six people between 1776 and 1777.

# dual federalism



**What it is:** when the state and federal governments have a clear separation

**How it works:** In the early days of the American government, there was more of a clear separation between what the national government could do and what the state governments could do. In dual federalism, like in a layer cake, the two levels of government are separate and distinct, with their own powers and autonomy. Over time, as the nation expanded, the reality became more complicated and the powers of each level of government grew. It became nearly impossible to have a clear separation between the two, which led to cooperative federalism.

**How it is used:** In a **dual federalism** government, the federal government is responsible for taxing income, while the state government is responsible for taxing goods and services.

# elite democracy



**What it is:** a theory where the true power lies with the wealthy and influential classes of society

**How it works:** In a democracy, the people hold the power. Under the theory of elite democracy, the true power comes from those with money and status. This theory states that this class of people has a disproportionate amount of power and influence over the policymaking process. Due to the increasing costs of elections, political leaders rely on those with money to support their campaigns. The theory of elite democracy says this connection leads to political leaders making decisions based on what the wealthy want, so that they can maintain their positions in the government, ultimately giving the elite class a greater amount of power.

**How it is used:** Some political scientists argue that the United States has an **elite democracy** today, due to campaign financing and the fact that many people serving in public office are incredibly wealthy.

# enumerated powers



**What it is:** authority specifically given to the federal government by the Constitution

**How it works:** The Constitution outlines the powers of the national government in the United States. These are called enumerated powers, or sometimes expressed powers, as they're clearly expressed in the Constitution. These powers include Congress's power to coin money, declare war, borrow money, and levy taxes. Enumerated powers also include the president's power to appoint ambassadors and Supreme Court justices, as well as the Supreme Court's power to rule on issues of United States law.

**How it is used: Enumerated powers** can't be taken away from the United States government without an amendment to the Constitution.

# extradition



**What it is:** the policy of a state government handing over an individual to another state at the request of the governor

**How it works:** If someone commits a crime, flees to another state, and is then arrested by the police, that individual must be sent back to the state they fled if requested by that state's governor. This is called extradition, and the policy of extradition between the states can be found in article 4 of the Constitution, where the relations between state governments are outlined. Extradition is an important policy to guarantee that states don't discriminate against each other. The US also has extradition policies with other countries in the world in case criminals flee the country.

**How it is used:** When Billy was arrested in Ohio for a crime committed in Vermont, the nation's **extradition** policy ensured he was sent back to Vermont to stand trial.

# Federalists



**What it is:** a group of people who supported the ratification of the Constitution

**How it works:** During the Constitution's ratification process, the Anti-Federalists made arguments about why people should vote against the new government. The Federalists responded to these claims by writing *The Federalist Papers*. They argued that checks and balances, separation of powers, and voting would limit the power of the government. They also wrote that a large republic would be the best form of government to control the harmful effects of factions, groups of individuals driven by self-interest. In the end, the Federalists agreed to add a Bill of Rights so the Constitution could go into effect.

**How it is used:** Alexander Hamilton, James Madison, and John Jay were three **Federalists** who took up the charge arguing in favor of the original Constitution.

# Full Faith and Credit Clause



**What it is:** a constitutional clause ensuring that each state adheres to the laws in other states in matters of public acts, records, and judicial proceedings

**How it works:** Found in article 4 of the Constitution, the Full Faith and Credit Clause was put into effect to make sure the states treated each other fairly and with respect. The idea behind this clause was that each state must recognize and respect another state's processes. For example, if you are legally married in one state and then move to another, the new state must recognize your marriage even though your license was issued in a different state. Similarly, if you're convicted of a crime and sentenced to community service in one state and then move to another, you still have to complete your sentence.

**How it is used:** Under the **Full Faith and Credit Clause**, you cannot be arrested for driving in Texas with an Alabama driver's license.

# grants-in-aid



**What it is:** funds given to the states by the federal government to pay for programs and services

**How it works:** Oftentimes, the federal government will give money to the states to help with the execution of certain initiatives; this funding is called grants-in-aid and comes in different forms. Categorical grants are the most common and require that the money be spent on a specific policy. These can be competitive project grants, where the money is spent on a particular project, or formula grants, where the money is given based on certain formulaic factors, such as population or income level. Additionally, block grants are chunks of money given to the states to be used on a broad issue.

**How it is used:** Over the last one hundred years, **grants-in-aid** have increased substantially, with a peak of $1.13 trillion given to the states in 2021.

# implied powers



**What it is:** authority hinted at but not listed explicitly in the Constitution

**How it works:** Enumerated powers are the powers specifically listed in the Constitution, but the federal government has other powers that aren't specifically listed. Some of these are considered implied powers. Congress receives its implied powers through the Necessary and Proper Clause. The president's implied powers come from the Executive Vesting Clause, stating the executive power is vested in the president. The Supreme Court's ultimate power of judicial review is an implied power as well; for example, the Supreme Court can rule that something the government did on the basis of an implied power was unconstitutional.

**How it is used:** Congress's ability to institute a draft is an **implied power**, stemming from its constitutional power to raise and support the armed forces.

# individual rights



**What it is:** rights the government gives to the people

**How it works:** While natural rights are what people are all born with, individual rights are the rights that people are given by their government. These rights are protected by the government and, similar to natural rights, shouldn't be taken away without just cause. Individual rights in the United States include those listed in the Bill of Rights, such as the freedoms of speech and religion and the right to due process.

**How it is used:** In order for **individual rights** to be taken away, the government must follow due process.

# limited government



**What it is:** the government has only the power the Constitution gives it

**How it works:** To prevent the government from abusing its power, the Constitution places limits on what the national and state governments can do. Some of these limits forbid ex post facto laws, which are laws that retroactively make a legal act illegal; the granting of titles of nobility; the enforcement of religious tests for government officials; and the suspension of the right to a trial by jury. State governments also can't coin money, declare war, negotiate treaties, or tax imports or exports. Checks and balances, separation of powers, and the Bill of Rights also limit the power of the government.

**How it is used:** After experiencing what they believed to be an abuse of governmental power under Great Britain, the founding leaders wanted to ensure **limited government** in the new Constitution of the United States.

# majority rule with minority rights



**What it is:** the concept that although the bulk of a population makes the decisions, the smaller population's rights are protected

**How it works:** The founding leaders were concerned with a democracy trampling the rights and voices of those not in the majority. To protect those individuals, they promoted the idea of majority rule with minority rights. This idea is that the majority will always win in decision-making, but they can't have enough power to eliminate the rights of the minority. Minority rights will always be protected in a republic because the rights of all people are protected in a republic. The government doesn't have enough power to trample the rights of citizens.

**How it is used:** In Congress, the concept of **majority rule with minority rights** can be seen through the legislative process, with both members of the majority and minority parties being able to propose bills.

# New Federalism



**What it is:** a trend in federalism where the federal government gives powers back to the states

**How it works:** New Federalism (or devolution) has occurred on and off since President Ronald Reagan's administration in the 1980s. Under devolution, the federal government transfers responsibilities back to the states for things like welfare programs or education standards. Often, this shift happens with limited funding to the states, leading to economic problems. Devolution also includes limiting the powers given to the federal government over time. In the 1995 Supreme Court case *United States v. Lopez*, the Supreme Court limited Congress's powers under the Commerce Clause and gave some power of economic regulation back to the states.

**How it is used:** Under President Bill Clinton, the federal government began shifting the responsibility of social services back to the states, implementing **New Federalism**, and calling this time the "devolution revolution."

# nullification



**What it is:** the theory that a state can refuse to obey a federal law on the grounds that the state believes it's unconstitutional

**How it works:** Under the theory of nullification, states declare an act of the federal government as void if they don't believe the federal government has the authority to pass a law. A famous example of this was the nullification crisis in the 1830s when South Carolina refused to pay the new federal tariffs because the people believed the tariffs were unconstitutional. This instance ended with Congress passing the Force Bill, allowing the president to send the military to South Carolina to enforce this new law if the state continued to resist. Over the years, the Supreme Court has continually ruled against state nullification attempts.

**How it is used:** In 1957, the state of Arkansas attempted to use **nullification** to stop the enforcement of the ruling of *Brown v. Board of Education of Topeka*.

## participatory democracy

*people's involvement is essential for democracy*

**What it is:** a theory that states that people partaking in politics is critical to the success of a democracy

**How it works:** Participatory democracy is a theory that believes that the people hold the power and their participation in government is essential. Under this theory, people participate in the government through a variety of ways, including joining groups outside the government's control that then influence the government. These groups can be interest groups, labor unions, or political parties. People's participation demonstrates a strong civil society where the people care about working toward the common good. This, in turn, increases participation and the people's role in policymaking. Under this theory, the people hold the power, with policymakers looking to them and their participation to influence decision-making.

**How it is used:** Ballot initiatives and referendums are examples of **participatory democracy**, with the people directly influencing the legislative process.

## pluralist democracy

*groups hold the power*

**What it is:** a theory that emphasizes the role of groups in the policymaking process

**How it works:** Americans have always joined together with like-minded people to try and invoke change. The pluralist theory of democracy is rooted in the idea that these groups are competing for power in the policymaking process, which leaves all groups represented in the democracy. As groups compete, it leads to bargaining and compromise with no single group dominating. This theory expands into hyperpluralism when groups, like special interest groups, begin to dominate the policymaking process and then have all the control.

**How it is used:** The Civil Rights Act of 1964 is a great example of **pluralist democracy** in action, with multiple civil rights organizations such as the NAACP and the ACLU acting as key players in its passage.

# police powers

*a state's power to protect its citizens*

**What it is:** the power of state governments to protect citizens' health and safety and to promote the general welfare of citizens

**How it works:** Under police powers, state governments have the authority to pass laws that potentially limit the private rights of citizens to benefit the public good. This can include licensure laws for medical professionals and educators, vaccine requirements for certain professions, zoning laws for businesses, traffic regulations for safety, and many other issues. These laws might restrict the freedoms of some people, but they're seen as being necessary for the public good. States derive the right to enact police powers from the 10th Amendment, but these powers can't conflict with the federal law.

**How it is used:** During the COVID-19 pandemic, state governments exercised their **police powers** when issuing mask mandates and curfews.

# popular sovereignty

*the people have the power*

**What it is:** the government derives its power from those who live in the country

**How it works:** Popular sovereignty, similar to the concept of the consent of the governed, is the theory that the government receives its authority from the people. The government exists because its citizens allow it to exist. The people's consent gives legitimacy to the government and allows them to exercise their influence. An important component of popular sovereignty is that the people give their consent to the government through their participation, namely by voting for their representatives.

**How it is used: <u>Popular sovereignty</u>** is demonstrated in the Constitution with the first three words, "We the People," implying the people are the source of power for this government.

# preamble



**What it is:** the first paragraph of the Constitution outlining the goals of the United States government

**How it works:** The preamble outlines not only that the people are the source of power for the United States government but also what the major goals of the government are. Beginning with "We the People," the preamble goes on to state that this new government will strive to be one of unity, justice, order, defense, citizen welfare, and freedom. This powerful paragraph of the Constitution lets people know the government's intentions. It also helps to demonstrate the changes that needed to be made from the Articles of Confederation.

**How it is used:** The **<u>preamble</u>** states, "We the People of the United States, in Order to form a more perfect Union, establish Justice, insure domestic Tranquility, provide for the common defense, promote the general Welfare, and secure the Blessings of Liberty to ourselves and our Posterity, do ordain and establish this Constitution for the United States of America."

## Privileges and Immunities Clause



**What it is:** a policy that says states cannot favor citizens of another state without justification

**How it works:** The Privileges and Immunities Clause found in article 4 of the Constitution was implemented to create a sense of national unity by allowing for the travel between states without fear of discrimination. For example, a state can't implement a higher sales tax on goods for people who are traveling through the state. Additionally, the clause was passed in an effort to ensure states guaranteed the same rights to nonstate residents, and to allow for protection of things like property ownership and access to the legal system.

**How it is used:** The **Privileges and Immunities Clause** protects citizens from discrimination, but states can charge out-of-state tuition for public universities and colleges because nonresidents don't pay taxes in that state.

# republicanism

*people play an active role in the government*

**What it is:** the concept that a government is based on civic virtue and that the people play a pivotal role in its process

**How it works:** Republicanism is the idea that the people play an important role in their government system. Ultimately, the government should work toward the common good, and citizens should actively participate in the government. Deriving from the Latin *res publica*, republicanism demands that the government be a public matter with the people participating frequently. In article 4 of the Constitution, the concept of a republican form of government is guaranteed to each citizen at both the state and federal level.

**How it is used:** **Republicanism** rejects the concept of hereditary rule—where power is passed down from one generation to the next.

# reserved powers

*powers of the states*

**What it is:** authorities that are reserved to the states and only the states

**How it works:** The 10th Amendment says that all powers not specifically given to the national government in the Constitution, and not specifically denied to the states, are reserved for the states. These reserved powers are not for the national government and include a state's ability to determine licensure for different professions and marriages, to conduct elections, to determine standards for education, and to regulate intrastate commerce.

**How it is used:** Determining the qualifications of voters, such as through registration requirements and voter ID laws, is a **reserved power** of the states.

## revenue sharing

*tax dollars from the federal government*

**What it is:** the process of the national government giving a portion of the taxes collected back to the states

**How it works:** The federal government collects taxes every year. Revenue sharing takes place when the federal government gives a portion of those taxes back to the states based on a predetermined calculation. This money is given to the states to help them offset the cost of programs and services in the state. Today, revenue sharing mainly takes the form of block grants, where the state is given a lump sum of money to spend at their discretion.

**How it is used: Revenue sharing** is a component of New Federalism, as it gives back to the states, further decentralizing the national government.

## rule of law

*no one is above the law*

**What it is:** no person, including government officials, is exempt from the law

**How it works:** Rule of law is an important concept in a republic. It strives to have all laws be applied consistently and fairly to all people. Rule of law also attempts to limit corruption from political officials by stating that they aren't exempt from the law. If a government official breaks the law, they'll be tried and punished just like anyone else. Rule of law allows the people of a nation to feel confident that everyone is held to the same standard and that the government is seeking to protect the rights of all people.

**How it is used:** In an attempt to ensure the **rule of law**, the Constitution allows for the president, vice president, and federal judges and justices to be impeached for crimes, which could potentially end in their removal from office.

# separation of powers



**What it is:** the political principle of dividing the authority of the government into three separate and distinct branches

**How it works:** In an effort to keep the national government from harnessing too much power, the founding leaders at the Constitutional Convention decided to enact the political philosophy of separation of powers, promoted by the philosopher Montesquieu. They created three separate branches of government. Each branch has its own unique powers: The legislative branch makes the laws, the executive branch enforces the laws, and the judicial branch interprets the laws. All are powers integral to the government, but by separating them, it keeps a single branch from becoming too powerful.

**How it is used:** First used in ancient Greece, the principle of **separation of powers** is widely used in the governments around the world today.

# Shays' Rebellion



**What it is:** a farmers' rebellion beginning in Massachusetts in 1786 that highlighted the weaknesses of the Articles of Confederation

**How it works:** After the Revolutionary War, American farmers found themselves in debt. State governments also found themselves in debt, so they increased taxes. Farmers who couldn't pay down their debts, or afford their taxes, lost their land and their livelihoods. Under the leadership of Daniel Shays and others, some of these farmers decided to rebel. Massachusetts couldn't stop the rebellion because the militia consisted of farmers. Congress, under the Articles of Confederation, also couldn't interfere because it had no military and no way to raise funds. Shays' Rebellion highlighted the dangers of a weak central government and was a major catalyst for the Constitutional Convention.

**How it is used:** Ultimately, **Shays' Rebellion** was stopped when the governor of Massachusetts hired mercenaries from other states to stop the farmers in their attempt to raid an arsenal.

## Supremacy Clause

*the Constitution is the ultimate law*

**What it is:** a clause in the Constitution stating that the Constitution and the laws made by the national government are the supreme law of the land

**How it works:** In article 6 of the Constitution, the Supremacy Clause provides the foundation that the federal government is more powerful than the state governments. Although state governments have the power to make laws, they can't make laws that conflict with the federal government. If there is ever a conflict, the federal law supersedes the state law. Sometimes, there are laws in conflict. For example, marijuana is an illegal drug according to the federal government, but many states have legalized its use. In this instance, the federal government is allowing the states to be a laboratory of democracy, testing the law to see its effects.

**How it is used:** In the 1819 Supreme Court case *McCulloch v. Maryland*, the court ruled that Maryland couldn't tax the federal bank in its state because this action violated the **Supremacy Clause**.

# Chapter 3

# THE LEGISLATIVE BRANCH

Article 1 of the Constitution outlines the powers and duties of the US government's legislative branch. The legislative branch is the United States' lawmaking body, consisting of the House of Representatives, with 435 members, and the Senate, with 100 members. Together, these 535 individuals make up Congress, and they make public policy for the nation, including laws, government programs, services, and policies on a wide range of issues. The founding leaders believed in legislative supremacy, or the idea that the lawmaking branch should have the most power. This is why article 1 is the longest article in the Constitution. Members of Congress are the only federal government representatives who are directly elected by the people. As such, they're closer to the people. The founders believed that this was why Congress should have more power, since a republic is meant to represent the people.

This chapter focuses entirely on the legislative branch. From the powers legislative branch is granted in the Constitution, to the limitations on this power, to the vocabulary used in the bill-making process, these pages attempt to give you a deeper understanding of the intricacies of the legislative branch in American government.

# 17th Amendment



**What it is:** an amendment to the Constitution that changed the election of senators to direct election by the people

**How it works:** When the Constitution was first ratified, it called for the senators to be selected by the state governments. Over time, this system led to corruption, with the Senate gaining the nickname the millionaires' club, as it seemed to serve only the interests of big business and the rich. In 1913, during the Progressive Era, the 17th Amendment was passed, which transferred the election of senators to the people. This amendment gave the people greater access to the government by allowing them to select all their congressional representatives.

**How it is used:** The **17th Amendment** was proposed by Senator Joseph Bristow of Kansas in 1911.

# advice and consent



**What it is:** the power of the Senate to approve or deny presidential appointments and treaties

**How it works:** Checks and balances work to keep one branch of government from becoming too powerful. Advice and consent is one of the Senate's checks on the president and the executive branch. The president has the power to negotiate treaties and appoint ambassadors, Supreme Court justices, other federal judges, and other public officials. Many of these appointments require a confirmation in the Senate. A simple majority of the Senate is all that's required to approve these presidential actions, but it serves to give the legislative branch a voice in the executive and judicial branches.

**How it is used:** The Senate used its power of **advice and consent** when confirming the most recent Supreme Court justice appointed to the bench.

# appropriations bills



**What it is:** a bill that grants federal bureaucratic departments and agencies permission to spend money

**How it works:** Congress has the power of the purse, meaning it controls the spending of the federal government and the executive branch. To enact that spending, an appropriations bill must be passed through both houses of Congress. This action gives Congress control over what money is being spent where. Appropriations are a fundamental component of the budget process, as Congress can increase or decrease spending for discretionary programs. Each year, twelve appropriations bills are passed to fund the government. If Congress can't agree on these bills, it can lead to a government shutdown.

**How it is used:** In 2025, a government shutdown occurred because members of Congress couldn't pass an **appropriations bill** for the 2026 fiscal year.

# authorization



**What it is:** the congressional power to create, maintain, and cancel federal agencies

**How it works:** Congress has the power to establish federal departments and agencies as well as make changes to them or eliminate them entirely. This power is authorization, and it's typically handled by congressional committees dedicated to certain policy areas. An authorization must be in place for an agency to exist. Authorization also extends to allowing certain programs, activities, or projects to continue. Authorization by itself doesn't provide funding, but authorization must exist for an appropriations bill to be passed.

**How it is used:** The National Defense Authorization Act, which establishes certain military policies and authorizes nuclear weapons programs, is a type of military **authorization** that Congress renews each year.

# bill



**What it is:** before a law is approved, it's presented before the legislative branch as a bill

**How it works:** In the lawmaking process, members of Congress work to pass bills through both houses so that they become laws. Bills are the rough drafts of laws that are then edited, investigated, and debated by Congress. Most bills don't become laws. There are more than ten thousand bills proposed each two-year term of Congress, but fewer than 7 percent of proposed bills typically become laws. Bills can be about anything within the powers of Congress. To read more about how bills become laws, see the *legislative process* entry in this chapter.

**How it is used:** Anyone can see all of the **bills** that Congress is working on by going to Congress's website.

# Census



**What it is:** the official population tally conducted by the federal government every ten years

**How it works:** Article 1 of the Constitution states a census must be completed every ten years in the United States. The Census is important for a number of reasons: It gives insight into the current demographics of the country, but it also plays a pivotal role in determining how many representatives each state will have in the House of Representatives and how many electors each state will have in the Electoral College. After the Census is completed, reapportionment and redistricting take place.

**How it is used:** Workers collect data for the **Census** by encouraging people to complete it online and, in many cases, by going door-to-door.

# cloture



**What it is:** the procedure for ending debate in the Senate and voting on a bill

**How it works:** The House of Representatives and the Senate have different rules for debating bills. In the Senate, senators can use the filibuster, a method for delaying a vote. To end the filibuster, or debate in general, they need cloture. Cloture requires that three-fifths of senators vote to end the debate. This amounts to sixty senators agreeing to move forward. Most bills require a simple majority to pass, but almost all of them require cloture to move forward to a vote. If cloture isn't met, then the bill doesn't get voted on, essentially killing the bill.

**How it is used:** Senators didn't meet **cloture** on a recent infrastructure bill that would have increased funding for highways.

# conference committee



**What it is:** when a bill has been passed, this committee meets to discuss changes

**How it works:** After a bill has been approved in both the House of Representatives and the Senate, it goes to a conference committee. Each house of Congress has adjusted the bill and possibly added some amendments (changes). In a conference committee, members from both houses meet to discuss how they can combine the two versions of the bill. Once they've added all the changes from each house, they send the newly reconciled bill back to both the House of Representatives and the Senate to be voted on again. If it passes, it makes its way to the president's desk.

**How it is used:** When the Voting Rights Act of 1965 was in **conference committee**, it merged together the House and Senate versions to create a bipartisan bill that has been renewed multiple times by members of Congress.

# Congress



**What it is:** the legislative body of the United States government

**How it works:** The legislative branch of the United States government is made up of the two houses of Congress: the House of Representatives and the Senate. The job of Congress is to make the laws for the nation. Congress is seen as the branch that's closest to the people, as representatives are directly elected to represent their interests. Because of this, the founding leaders believed that Congress should have more power than the other branches but not enough to seize power. This is called legislative supremacy.

**How it is used: <u>Congress</u>** met this week to discuss new legislation to help veterans receive greater access to healthcare.

# congressional caucus



**What it is:** members of Congress with similar interests and values who form groups to promote their interests

**How it works:** Congress is made up of many different people. In an effort to focus their interests, members of Congress will form a caucus to have a voting bloc (a temporary combination of parties) on specific issues and to pursue shared goals. There are hundreds of caucuses in Congress, and many members of Congress are part of multiple caucus groups. Interests of these caucus groups cover many topics, including international relations, environmental concerns, social issues, and specific political ideology.

**How it is used:** The US Congressional Baseball **<u>Caucus</u>** met this week to continue their goal of fostering relationships across the aisle through a love of baseball.

# congressional oversight



**What it is:** the power of Congress to oversee the executive branch's implementation of laws

**How it works:** Most of the time, Congress creates laws but leaves the enforcement and rules of the law to the executive branch. Congress can, however, exercise oversight of the executive branch, where it holds hearings to monitor how departments and agencies are implementing the law. Congress does this to ensure the laws are consistent and fair, while also working to eliminate wasteful spending or fraud. If Congress believes that the federal agencies in charge of carrying out the law aren't acting in Congress's vision, it can limit future funding, end programs, or take other action.

**How it is used:** Using its power of **congressional oversight**, Congress held hearings to determine the impact of social media on America's youth.

# constituent



**What it is:** the citizens of their state or district that members of Congress represent

**How it works:** When members of Congress go to work, they're there to work toward the interests of their constituents. This is the greatest responsibility of Congress members, as the US is a representative democracy. Members of Congress inform constituents of major issues and correspond with them through regular newsletters and town hall meetings. Members of Congress are there to address concerns of constituents and to help them navigate the federal government. Constituents can always contact their representatives to express their opinions on what matters to them and how the representative should vote.

**How it is used:** A representative's **constituents** raised concerns about a law he was in favor of, leading him to change his vote.

# deficit spending



**What it is:** the process of spending more money than earning in revenue

**How it works:** In the United States, the federal government acquires money through taxation. It also spends an enormous amount of money annually on government programs and public goods. In fact, the federal government spends more than it brings in, which is called deficit spending. Each year, the government operates at a deficit and borrows money to make up for the money it doesn't have but is spending. All of these deficits make up the national debt.

**How it is used:** During the 2025 fiscal year, the federal government's **deficit** was $1.78 trillion, a 2 percent decrease from the 2024 fiscal year.

# delegate model



**What it is:** the model of representation by a member of Congress where they do what their constituents want

**How it works:** When members of Congress are deciding how to vote on bills, they sometimes use the delegate model of representation. This is where they act as a delegate for the people and vote based on what their constituents want rather than what they personally want. Oftentimes, members of Congress will use the delegate model on major issues that might affect their reelection efforts. They won't want to vote against what the majority of their constituents want if it's a hot-button issue that people care deeply about.

**How it is used:** A senator used the **delegate model** when voting on a polarizing environmental issue of great interest to their constituents and their state.

# discharge petition



**What it is:** a legislative tool in the House of Representatives that bypasses the committee steps that typically occur before a vote

**How it works:** A discharge petition is a way to force a bill out of committee before the committee has finished editing it or voting on it if the bill has been delayed for more than thirty days. The discharge petition sends the bill straight to the floor of the House to be voted on. This tool is used only in the House of Representatives. Members of the House serve for two years, so they have limited time to enact legislation. Discharge petitions allow them to speed up the legislative process if needed.

**How it is used:** A majority of members of the House of Representatives signed a **discharge petition** to force an important bill out of committee so they can vote on it.

# discretionary spending



**What it is:** government costs that are flexible and can change from year to year

**How it works:** When Congress is looking at the federal budget proposed by the president, it has certain things it has to spend money on (see *mandatory spending* in this chapter), and everything else is considered discretionary spending. Congress can change how much is spent on major issues and departments through this spending. Programs that fall under discretionary spending include the military and defense, education, housing, social services, and transportation. Spending doesn't have to be the same from year to year, so Congress can increase or decrease the budget for certain areas of the government if it chooses.

**How it is used:** In general, about half of **discretionary spending** goes to defense spending, with $850 billion requested for fiscal year 2025.

# earmark



**What it is:** money that's specifically allocated to a certain district or state

**How it works:** When Congress passes spending bills, or appropriations, it's common to see earmarks included. These earmarks are funds that are designated for a specific project in a certain area. This could be a research grant, infrastructure project, or any other specific congressional project. Earmarks outline exactly how the money should be spent and where the money is going. They exist for a targeted reason, most of the time to help a particular congressional district or region. Many earmarks draw criticism, as they cost large amounts of money but don't benefit large numbers of people.

**How it is used:** An example of an **earmark** that would cost a lot and benefit very few people is the Gravina Island Bridge (or the Bridge to Nowhere), which was supposed to be a bridge in Alaska that connected remote areas and was estimated to cost more than $300 million.

# Federal Reserve



**What it is:** the central banking institution for the United States

**How it works:** Nicknamed the Fed, the Federal Reserve System is an independent institution that works for the federal government and reports to Congress. The US president appoints and the Senate confirms new members to the Board of Governors, the governing body of the Federal Reserve. These seven individuals help with the operation of the twelve Federal Reserve banks across the country and enact monetary policy to help the economy. The Federal Reserve also works to create financial stability in the nation, supervises and regulates the nation's banks, and monitors payment systems in the country.

**How it is used:** The **Federal Reserve** collects and analyzes information and data about the United States' economic conditions, which it then uses to help stabilize the economy.

# filibuster



**What it is:** the process of speaking at length to delay the vote on a bill in the Senate

**How it works:** One of the differences between the debate process in the House and the Senate is that the Senate has the opportunity to filibuster. Filibustering is a tactic that representatives use when they're attempting to delay a vote because they don't want the bill to pass. To end a filibuster, the Senate must meet cloture, where sixty of the senators agree to stop and vote. When filibustering, a senator must remain standing and speak without taking breaks. Today, simply declaring an intention to filibuster can be enough to stop a bill.

**How it is used:** The longest **filibuster** lasted for just over twenty-four hours when Strom Thurmond spoke at length in an effort to stop the Civil Rights Act of 1957.

# fiscal policy



**What it is:** Congress's power to stabilize the economy through taxation and government spending

**How it works:** When the US economy slows too much or grows too quickly, Congress will sometimes attempt to help by changing taxation and spending policies. During a recession, when the economy slows down and unemployment rises, Congress might lower taxes, so people have more money to spend. It can also increase government spending to create jobs. When the economy grows too quickly and there's high inflation, Congress might increase taxes to take money out of the economy or decrease government spending to take pressure off the economy. Congress can use these tools at any time, depending on the current economic climate.

**How it is used:** **Fiscal policy** is used to promote a strong economy by encouraging employment, price stability, and economic growth.

# gerrymandering



**What it is:** the policy of redrawing the boundaries of congressional districts to benefit one party over another

**How it works:** Typically, after the Census has completed the population count, state legislatures begin to redraw their district lines. Most states practice gerrymandering, where the majority party creates districts that advantage their party and allow them to maintain power. Two tactics of gerrymandering are packing and cracking. Packing is when you put as many of the opposing party as possible into a small number of districts. Cracking is when you spread out the opposing party so they become minorities in all districts. Gerrymandering isn't considered unconstitutional when party affiliation is used to draw district lines, but racial gerrymandering is considered unconstitutional.

**How it is used:** Republicans and Democrats both use **gerrymandering** as a way to gain an advantage in the House of Representatives.

# government shutdown



**What it is:** what happens when members of Congress can't pass a budget

**How it works:** Every year, members of Congress must approve the federal budget. This is a complicated process, but the budget bill is similar to all others in that it has to pass through both houses of Congress. If it fails to do that by a certain deadline, the government will shut down. All nonessential federal personnel will be furloughed or sent home without pay. Some individuals will work but won't be paid. Certain government services will be unavailable, as the government hasn't approved spending. Once the budget is approved, the government will begin operating again.

**How it is used: Government shutdowns** can have significant impacts on the economy and the lives of American citizens.

# House of Representatives



**What it is:** the chamber of Congress closest to the people

**How it works:** Representation in the House of Representatives is based on population, with each member (435 in total) representing a congressional district within a state. As such, the House represents more people, thereby making it closer to the people. To be a representative, you must be at least twenty-five years old, a citizen of the US for at least seven years, and a resident of the state you represent. Members are directly elected by the people every two years and can be reelected as many times as their constituents want.

**How it is used:** Each congressional member of the **House of Representatives** represents about 760,000 people.

# impeachment



**What it is:** the power of Congress to try and remove certain government officials from their positions

**How it works:** Impeachment is a legislative check on the executive and judicial branches. The president, vice president, Supreme Court justices, and federal judges can all be impeached for treason, bribery, or other high crimes or misdemeanors. The House of Representatives draws up the articles of impeachment if it believes an official has committed a crime. Impeachment trials take place in the Senate, where two-thirds of senators must vote to remove the official from office. To date, three presidents have been impeached four times, with none being removed from office. But fifteen federal judges have been impeached and eight have been removed from office.

**How it is used:** President Andrew Johnson was one vote shy of being removed from office after his **impeachment** trial in 1868.

# joint committee



**What it is:** a congressional committee that has members from both the House of Representatives and the Senate

**How it works:** A large part of the legislative process involves committees. A joint committee of Congress has members from both chambers coming together to work on certain issues. Currently, there are four permanent joint committees. Their focuses are on taxation, printing, the Library of Congress, and economic matters. Joint committees allow both houses to work together on important issues that they care about. Often, they'll perform administrative duties and conduct investigations for informational or oversight purposes. They also promote cross-chamber collaboration.

**How it is used:** The **Joint Committee** on Printing is one of the oldest committees in Congress, and it oversees the U.S. Government Publishing Office, which prints the documents that members of Congress rely on to do their work.

# legislative process



**What it is:** the process through which members of Congress work to create laws

**How it works:** The legislative process begins with a proposal for a new law (a bill) from any member of Congress. The bill is then assigned to a committee in whichever house it was proposed in. In the committee, members develop the bill. If it passes through the committee, it goes to the floor to be debated and voted on by all members of either the House or the Senate. Upon passing, it goes to the other chamber and repeats the process. If the bill makes it through both houses, it goes to the president to either be signed into law or vetoed.

**How it is used:** Although people expect a speedier system, the founding leaders designed the **legislative process** to be slow and deliberate to keep frivolous laws from being passed.

# logrolling



**What it is:** the process of members of Congress trading votes to get legislation passed

**How it works:** In Congress, deals sometimes have to be made in order for legislation to get passed. Logrolling is a strategy members of Congress use to get their bills passed, where members will agree to vote for each other's bills in an effort to secure as many votes as possible. This is a quid pro quo, where one member votes for someone else's bill to gain that person's vote on their own bill. Logrolling is often associated with pork barrel legislation.

**How it is used:** **Logrolling** can help facilitate compromise among members of Congress, but it is frequently used to increase (often unnecessary) spending through the trading of votes to approve spending projects in a Congress member's home state.

# majority leader



**What it is:** the selected member to represent the larger party of each house in Congress

**How it works:** The House of Representatives and the Senate both have a majority leader. This person is a member of the majority political party and is selected by the party to represent them. In the House, this person is second-in-command to the Speaker of the House. In the Senate, the majority leader represents their party as a spokesperson and schedules bills to be discussed on the Senate floor. The majority leader in both houses works to promote the strategy of their political party as they move through the legislative process.

**How it is used:** The **majority leader** represented their party during the floor debate for a bill this week by stating that their party wasn't in favor of this piece of legislation.

# mandatory spending



**What it is:** the funds that the government is required to spend on entitlement programs

**How it works:** During the annual budget process, Congress can make changes to the discretionary spending budget. Congress doesn't, however, need to make changes to the mandatory spending budget, though it can through new legislation. Mandatory spending goes toward ongoing programs that have spending levels determined typically through eligibility requirements and payment formulas. Items paid for through mandatory spending include entitlement programs such as Social Security, Medicare, and Medicaid; welfare programs; and veterans' benefits. The interest on the federal debt can also be mandatory spending.

**How it is used:** Approximately 60 percent of the money spent by Congress is spent on **mandatory spending** items, including $1.5 trillion on Social Security, $942 billion on Medicare, and $952 billion on the national debt's interest in fiscal year 2025.

# minority leader



**What it is:** the selected member to represent the smaller party of each house of Congress

**How it works:** The House of Representatives and the Senate both have a minority leader. This person is a member of the minority political party and is selected by the party to represent them. They serve as a spokesperson for the ideals of their party and are called upon to represent the party during full chamber debates. Although they don't have as much power as the majority leader, they do serve an important role in maintaining the voice of the minority party during the legislative process. Oftentimes, they'll work with the majority leader to find compromise.

**How it is used:** The **<u>minority leader</u>** in the Senate worked with their party members to propose a bill that aligned with their political beliefs.

## monetary policy

*managing the money supply*

**What it is:** policies enacted by the Federal Reserve to influence the economy

**How it works:** The Federal Reserve is the central bank of the United States. It's an independent agency, although Congress maintains oversight of the institution. Monetary policy is put into effect when the Federal Reserve uses its tools to influence the economy, predominantly by setting the interest rates for banks to use when lending money. During times of inflation, the Federal Reserve increases interest rates to keep more money out of the economy, as people won't borrow as much with a high interest rate. During a recession, the Federal Reserve decreases interest rates to encourage people to borrow and spend money.

**How it is used:** The primary goal of **<u>monetary policy</u>** is to promote a healthy economy with stable prices and high employment.

## Necessary and Proper Clause

*implied powers of Congress*

**What it is:** the clause in the Constitution that gives Congress its implied powers

**How it works:** The Necessary and Proper Clause grants Congress the power to enact laws that are necessary to carry out its enumerated powers. This clause, often called the Elastic Clause, stretches the power of Congress to allow it to accomplish more than just what is listed in the Constitution. Originally criticized for giving too much power to Congress, the Necessary and Proper Clause allows Congress to adapt over time. The Supreme Court case *McCulloch v. Maryland* ruled that anything that's within the scope of congressional power and that's needed is constitutional under the Necessary and Proper Clause.

**How it is used:** Congress used the **Necessary and Proper Clause** to create the federal banking system, as the system is needed to help Congress carry out its taxation and commerce powers.

# omnibus bill



**What it is:** a bill made up of smaller bills relating to the same topic

**How it works:** An omnibus bill takes multiple smaller bills and compiles them into one larger bill to be voted on as a whole. Most often, this tactic is used with regard to spending bills. This is done in an effort to get the bill passed and to save time as deadlines approach, especially if a government shutdown is a possible outcome. This type of bill has been met with some criticism, as some people say that legislators include riders (additions to a bill) in bills that increase government spending.

**How it is used: Omnibus bills** were passed in both 2023 and 2024 to help with funding government agencies and to avoid a government shutdown.

# override



**What it is:** Congress's power to overturn a presidential veto

**How it works:** In the legislative process, the president is the final stop after a bill has made its way through Congress. The president determines whether a bill should become law. If the president doesn't want the bill to be a law, they can veto it. If this happens, the bill is sent back to Congress. Congress can override the veto, but this requires a two-thirds majority vote in both houses. Although rare, this important check on presidential power has been used a number of times throughout history.

**How it is used:** Congress used its power to **override** a presidential veto when it passed the War Powers Resolution of 1973 over President Richard Nixon's veto.

# policy gridlock



**What it is:** used to describe a state of increased partisanship that keeps Congress from making laws

**How it works:** In order for bills to become laws, members of Congress must compromise and come to agreements. As society becomes more partisan—meaning people strongly adhere to a political party—this becomes more difficult. Members of Congress can't see eye to eye on many issues, particularly ones their constituents are passionate about. This oftentimes leads to policy gridlock, when policymaking slows down, sometimes at a complete standstill. This is also referred to as a political stalemate. Policy gridlock can result in consequences such as government shutdowns and public dissent.

**How it is used: Policy gridlock** frequently occurs when there's a divided government, meaning there are different majority parties in Congress and the presidency.

# politico model



**What it is:** the model of representation where a member of Congress serves the interests of their constituents and also themselves

**How it works:** When a member of Congress is making decisions, they consider a number of factors. When they make decisions based on what their constituents want and in their own self-interest, it's considered the politico model of representation. This is a combination of the delegate and trustee models of representation. Most members of Congress use this model of representation, considering what their constituents want on larger issues and using their own expertise on matters of little importance to their constituents.

**How it is used:** The representative used the **politico model** of representation when she voted for a bill that would provide jobs in her district, making her constituents happy, while voting against another bill about government spending, using her previous experience.

# pork barrel legislation

*spending bills for hyper-specific, localized projects*

**What it is:** a bill that includes funds allocated toward a specialized project to benefit a representative's district

**How it works:** Pork barrel legislation, sometimes just simply called pork, happens when members of Congress direct money to a project for their own benefit. This is typically done to gain an advantage in an election by giving money to a special interest group or to a congressional district. The money spent on pork barrel legislation usually benefits only one group of people. Most people don't approve of this type of spending, as it's viewed as trading money for votes.

**How it is used:** An example of **pork barrel legislation** is the infamous "Bridge to Nowhere" in Alaska, where more than $300 million was spent to build a bridge to connect a small island of fifty people with the mainland.

# president of the Senate

*presiding officer of the Senate*

**What it is:** the person who oversees the Senate during debates and votes

**How it works:** The president of the Senate is the individual who ensures that debates in the Senate are fair. This position is always occupied by the vice president. This is the vice president's only constitutional responsibility, other than being in line for the presidential succession. The president of the Senate can't participate in debates or vote, except to cast a tiebreaking vote. Additionally, they oversee the receiving and official casting of Electoral College votes from the states during a presidential election. Today, the vice president rarely presides over the Senate. Instead, senior-ranking members of the majority party rotate as presiding officers.

**How it is used:** The **president of the Senate** cast the tiebreaking vote during the appointment hearing of the secretary of defense.

# president pro tempore of the Senate

*vice president of the Senate*

**What it is:** the person who presides over the Senate in the absence of the president of the Senate

**How it works:** The president pro tempore is a largely ceremonial position, traditionally held by the longest-serving member of the majority party. The person in this role oversees the Senate when the president of the Senate can't be in attendance. The president pro tempore can also sign legislation and administer oaths of office. They cannot, however, cast a tiebreaking vote. Today, the president pro tempore rarely presides over the Senate. Instead, senior-ranking members of the majority party rotate as presiding officers.

**How it is used:** John Tyler is the only president to have served as **president pro tempore** of the Senate.

# quorum

*minimum number*

**What it is:** the smallest total number of members that must be present to begin a congressional session

**How it works:** According to the Constitution, Congress can't conduct official business unless a quorum has been met. The minimum number of members required is a majority of the House. The Senate has 100 members, so the quorum is set at 51 members. The House of Representatives has 435 members, so the quorum is set at 218. Quorum is typically counted only during a vote. Members of Congress generally operate as if quorum is met unless a member specifically asks for a quorum count.

**How it is used:** The senator asked for a **quorum** count to slow down proceedings and to have more time to negotiate with their fellow members.

# reapportionment



**What it is:** the process of redistributing seats in the House of Representatives based on new data from the Census

**How it works:** Reapportionment happens every ten years after the Census once the new population count is finished. These changes in state populations create a need to reallocate the seats in the House of Representatives, which are based on population. Each district in the House should be of equal population. As people move from state to state and the population shifts, reapportionment needs to take place to maintain fairness in representation. As a result, some states gain seats, some lose seats, and some maintain the same number. Reapportionment also affects the number of electoral votes a state has during presidential elections.

**How it is used:** After **reapportionment** based on the United States Census 2020, seven states lost a seat in the House of Representatives, while five states gained one seat each, and one state gained two seats.


# reconciliation bills



**What it is:** a bill that can avoid the supermajority vote in the Senate through a complicated process

**How it works:** A reconciliation bill is a way to fast-track pieces of legislation, particularly regarding the budget. In the Senate, a reconciliation bill requires only a simple majority (fifty-one votes), removing the need to meet cloture (sixty votes). This allows for budget-related items to be passed faster. This type of bill also allows for changes to be made to mandatory spending items and the federal debt limit. The reconciliation process begins when members of Congress include reconciliation instructions in a budget resolution, directing committees to meet specific revenue and spending targets.

**How it is used:** <u>**Reconciliation bills**</u> throughout history include Bill Clinton's Deficit Reduction Act and George W. Bush's tax cuts.

# redistricting



**What it is:** the process of redrawing congressional districts, typically after the Census and reapportionment

**How it works:** Although the redistricting process typically occurs after reapportionment, it can happen whenever a state wishes depending on its laws. As states gain and lose seats due to population shifts, they need to redraw their district lines to accommodate for the changes. Even states that don't have any changes to the number of districts tend to redraw their district lines, as people move within a state and the state needs to create districts with more even populations. State legislatures are the ones who draw the maps in most states. Many states also employ the tactic of gerrymandering to gain a political advantage.

**How it is used:** In 2025, Republicans and Democrats have both begun the process of **redistricting** in an effort to win control of the House of Representatives in the 2026 midterm election.

# rescissions



**What it is:** a piece of legislation that formally cancels funding that had previously been approved by Congress

**How it works:** Rescissions are sometimes enacted in an effort to align current government spending with the ideology in power, as governments change political parties. The president can propose rescissions (or cuts) in previously approved spending for certain government agencies, but Congress must approve them. After the president requests the cancellation of funds, the Office of Management and Budget freezes the funds for forty-five days while

Congress considers the rescissions. Congress can then pass a bill enacting the rescissions. If Congress doesn't act within the forty-five-day window, the president must release the funds to the government agencies.

**How it is used:** In 2025, a major **rescissions** bill was passed that eliminated previously allocated money for foreign aid and public broadcasting.

# resolution



**What it is:** a type of bill passed by Congress that typically doesn't carry the weight of law

**How it works:** A congressional resolution can take one of three shapes: simple, concurrent, or joint. A simple resolution is a document expressing the thoughts of a member of Congress or handling internal business of one of the chambers. A concurrent resolution requires approval from both houses of Congress but is not a law; these are typically for things that affect both houses and their daily operations. A joint resolution goes through the same steps as a bill and can become law; the exception to this is a joint resolution for a proposed amendment to the Constitution.

**How it is used:** Recently, a **resolution** was passed in the Senate, selecting the secretary of the Senate.

# revenue bills



**What it is:** the bills that collect funds for the federal government through taxation

**How it works:** The founding leaders were fearful of the government's taxation power after their experience with Great Britain, so they required that revenue bills must be proposed in the House of Representatives, as it's closest to the people. The purpose of revenue bills is to acquire money for the government so it can provide programs and services to the people as needed. Revenue is mainly generated through taxes, with income tax providing the majority of the government's revenue. The income tax was established through the 16th Amendment to the Constitution and subsequent acts of Congress that established the tax code.

**How it is used:** Although **revenue bills** must originate in the House of Representatives, they still must make it through both houses of Congress to become a law.

# rider



**What it is:** any addition to a bill that's not original to the bill itself

**How it works:** A rider is an amendment to a bill, often not related to the topic of the bill. Riders are often added to appropriations (spending) bills and sometimes are for pork barrel legislation or earmarks. A bill that has a lot of riders is called a Christmas tree bill, as the riders act as ornaments to the bill itself. Riders are added to bills that will be passed, like spending bills, because they wouldn't otherwise pass on their own.

**How it is used:** Some **riders**, known as poison pills, are attached to bills to make the bill fail.

# Rules Committee



**What it is:** a committee in the House of Representatives that establishes the rules for debates

**How it works:** The House of Representatives consists of 435 voting members. With so many voices, it's important to have rules established when debating over bills; hence, the Rules Committee (formally called the Committee on Rules) was established. Before a bill can be debated on the floor of the House, it must go to the Rules Committee. It's decided there if the bill will have an open rule, meaning if it will allow amendments, and how long the debate will last. The Rules Committee also determines the schedule of bills to be discussed.

**How it is used:** The **Rules Committee** is also called the Speaker's Committee, as the Speaker of the House uses it to wield tremendous power.

## safe seats

*secure spots in Congress*

**What it is:** districts in Congress that aren't expected to be flipped by the other party in an election

**How it works:** During congressional elections, many seats in Congress are considered safe if in the previous election, they were won by a large majority. This means that political parties and their leadership don't worry about losing those seats to the opposite party. They can factor these seats into their strategy to maintain power and instead focus on seats that had a closer margin between candidates. Additionally, the person who holds that seat can feel confident in their ability to win the election and may not spend as much time and energy campaigning.

**How it is used:** According to recent polling, there are 165 **safe seats** for Democrats and 189 safe seats for Republicans going into the 2026 election.

## select committee

*special group*

**What it is:** a committee in Congress that exists to focus on special issues and is often temporary

**How it works:** Select committees in Congress are focused on current issues that affect the country. Most of them aren't permanent committees and will dissolve after the issue has been resolved. Select committees typically conduct investigations into major issues of the time. In the past, these committees have investigated the assassinations of President John F. Kennedy and Martin Luther King Jr. and the Watergate scandal, which ultimately led to the resignation of President Richard Nixon.

**How it is used:** Some **select committees** are permanent, like the U.S. Senate Special Committee on Aging, which looks into matters related to older Americans.

## Senate



**What it is:** the legislative body of Congress based on equal representation

**How it works:** The Senate was created to be the more enlightened body within Congress. Senators' terms are six years, allowing them to focus on big picture issues. Representing their entire state gives senators a wide range of perspectives to consider. To be a senator, you must be thirty years old, a US citizen for at least nine years, and a resident of the state you represent. The Senate is considered a continuous body, with only one-third of its members up for reelection at a time. Every state is guaranteed two senators. The current size of the Senate is one hundred members.

**How it is used:** Originally, members of the **Senate** were elected by the state legislatures.

## Speaker of the House



**What it is:** the presiding officer of the House of Representatives

**How it works:** The Speaker of the House is the most powerful position in all of Congress. This individual is selected by the majority party in the House. Their duties include giving members permission to speak, keeping order, and enforcing the rules established by the Rules Committee during debates. As the head of the majority party in the larger chamber of Congress, this individual wields a great deal of power in the policymaking process. The Speaker of the House is also second in line for the presidency, per the Presidential Succession Act.

**How it is used:** The **Speaker of the House** plays an important role in determining who serves on which committee in the House of Representatives, thereby giving their party a distinct advantage.

# standing committee



**What it is:** a group that's established in Congress and won't dissolve

**How it works:** Standing committees are where the bulk of work in Congress takes place. After a bill has been proposed, it will be assigned to a standing committee, where the committee will take action on the bill. In the committee, members will conduct research and interviews on the need for such a law and the possible effects of such legislation. They'll mark up (edit) the bill to adjust it as they see fit. After they've finished working on a bill, they'll vote to bring it to the full chamber. Most bills die in committee.

**How it is used: Standing committees** focus on broad issues that cover a wide range of topics, while their subcommittees dive deeper into specific issues.

# trustee model



**What it is:** a model of representation in Congress where representatives make decisions based on their knowledge

**How it works:** When members of Congress make decisions, they consider many factors. Those who act as a trustee to the people make decisions based on their own knowledge of the issue and expertise. Trustees don't hesitate to vote against their constituents (the people they represent in their home state) if they feel that they know better. The idea behind this model of representation is that the representative has been selected as a trustee of the people because of their knowledge and experience. As such, they make their own decisions and aren't greatly influenced by their constituents.

**How it is used:** Going against their constituents' wishes, the representative used the **trustee model** when they voted for a piece of legislation based on their expertise in the field.

## Ways and Means Committee



**What it is:** a standing committee in the House of Representatives that focuses on revenue bills

**How it works:** The Ways and Means Committee (officially called the Committee on Ways and Means) is one of the most powerful committees in all of Congress. This committee is responsible for all revenue (or taxation) bills. Revenue bills must start in the House of Representatives, so this committee is essentially creating the laws on taxation for the nation. This committee also oversees the nation's debt as well as trade agreements and tariffs. Additionally, the revenue-related aspects of programs like Social Security and Medicare are under the purview of the Ways and Means Committee.

**How it is used:** The **Ways and Means Committee** recently held hearings regarding tax-exempt hospitals and how they're spending Americans' money.

## whip



**What it is:** a member of congressional leadership that serves as a liaison between leadership and other members of Congress

**How it works:** In both houses of Congress, there are a majority and a minority whip. These individuals work to communicate the legislative strategy and leadership's plans with those of the party they represent. They're mainly responsible for counting votes and ensuring that members of the party vote the way leadership wants them to on upcoming bills. Whips are elected by the members of their party at the beginning of the congressional session.

**How it is used:** Prior to voting on a bill, the majority and minority **whips** talked with members of their parties to make sure they were voting along party lines.

# Chapter 4

# THE EXECUTIVE BRANCH

The president is the most visible political figure in the American government. More Americans know who the president is than who represent them in Congress. Americans turn out to vote more in presidential elections than in any other elections. But most Americans don't understand the scope of the presidency, or of the executive branch as a whole. The executive branch enforces the nation's laws, working to carry out the policies enacted by Congress. The president is the head of this branch but is not the only member. Thousands of government workers help to execute the policies of the federal government. The president is the face of the branch, making decisions on major policy implementation, but they aren't the sole member of this part of the government.

This chapter focuses on the executive branch as a whole. The terms you'll find cover everything from the roles of the president and presidential power to the different departments, agencies, and commissions that execute policy. The policies that the executive branch enforce span every aspect of American life. This chapter works to bring to light the working of this complex, multifaceted branch of government.

# ambassador



**What it is:** a liaison between the US government and another country's government

**How it works:** As diplomats, ambassadors have an important role in international relations. They serve to represent the United States and its interests while working with another country's government. In their role, they promote the United States' foreign policy, while protecting American citizens abroad and creating strong international connections. Ambassadors work for the U.S. Department of State, are appointed by the president, and confirmed by the Senate. They live in the country they're the ambassador for. Additionally, the president, in their role as chief diplomat, receives foreign ambassadors.

**How it is used:** Between 1785 and 1789, Thomas Jefferson served as the American **ambassador** to France, a role that later influenced his beliefs on international affairs.

# budget



**What it is:** the outline of how much money the government spends

**How it works:** Each year, the president creates a budget to be proposed to Congress for approval. As the head of the executive branch, the president details how much money they believe each part of the government should receive. This money goes to departments and agencies to pay for employees as well as the execution of government programs. The president can propose changes to the federal budget, but it's up to Congress to approve these expenses.

**How it is used:** The **budget** for fiscal year 2025 was $7 trillion.

# bully pulpit



**What it is:** the president's ability to use their position to speak out on many issues

**How it works:** Presidents wield a lot of power, including their ability to reach large audiences of people. Presidents can communicate directly with the people to sway public opinion. Presidents who use their position to advocate for certain issues and gain support for different initiatives, especially legislation, are using the bully pulpit. Speeches, rallies, social media, press conferences, and media coverage are all ways for the president to use the bully pulpit to influence policy and promote their agenda.

**How it is used:** The term **bully pulpit** was first used by President Theodore Roosevelt, who used it to describe how the presidency can be a platform to champion important issues.

# bureaucracy



**What it is:** the departments, agencies, bureaus, and commissions that make up the executive branch

**How it works:** The president is the head of the executive branch, but they aren't the only person in that branch. The bureaucracy makes up the majority of this part of the federal government. Within the bureaucracy, there are the fifteen cabinet departments and numerous independent agencies, commissions, and government corporations. The role of the bureaucracy is to execute the laws passed by Congress. The president appoints individuals to oversee these departments, but the people who work in these departments aren't hired for their political affiliation.

**How it is used:** People who work in the **bureaucracy** are called bureaucrats.

# bureaucratic oversight



**What it is:** the government's powers to oversee the bureaucracy

**How it works:** Although the bureaucracy is independent in many ways from the politics of government, it's still important to have checks on its power. Each branch of government has ways to ensure that the bureaucracy isn't overstepping. The legislative branch controls the funds given to the bureaucracy and can hold oversight hearings. The president appoints the leaders of most of the bureaucracy and gives guidelines on how they expect the departments to be run. The courts can rule actions of the bureaucracy as unconstitutional. These checks, and others, allow for balance in the government.

**How it is used:** The bureaucracy has a great amount of power, as it determines the rules and execution of laws, which makes **bureaucratic oversight** incredibly important.

# cabinet



**What it is:** the heads of executive departments who form an advisory panel for the president

**How it works:** Each president has the power to appoint the heads of the fifteen executive departments. These individuals, called secretaries, plus the vice president and some other notable officials make up the president's cabinet. The secretaries keep the president informed of the major issues, as it's impractical for the president to know the everyday details of each department. The president also goes to the secretaries for their expertise when something related to their department comes across the president's desk. The president holds full cabinet meetings at their discretion and can meet with secretaries whenever they desire.

**How it is used:** The **cabinet** was created to provide the president with advisers to brief them on major policy areas in the United States.

# chief diplomat



**What it is:** the president's role in the federal government regarding international relations

**How it works:** Diplomacy is the act of countries negotiating with each other to reach a desired outcome. The president, in the role of chief diplomat, is the nation's top negotiator. As chief diplomat, the president is in charge of foreign relations and also represents the United States at international events. Included in this role are the president's powers to negotiate treaties, make agreements with foreign nations, send and receive ambassadors, and travel abroad. Aiding other countries in resolving conflicts, such as ending a war, is also within the chief diplomat's powers. The president also meets with leaders of foreign countries.

**How it is used:** President Theodore Roosevelt acted as **chief diplomat** when he worked to help end the Russo-Japanese War in 1905.

# chief executive



**What it is:** the president's role as the head of the entire executive branch

**How it works:** The executive branch of the federal government is made up of thousands of employees. This branch works to carry out the laws by imposing regulations and monitoring people's adherence to the laws. The president, as chief executive, is in charge of the entire branch. The chief executive hires people for different positions through appointments and sets the agenda for the implementation of laws within the branch. Additionally, the president's ability to issue executive orders and propose a federal budget fall under this role.

**How it is used:** When President Lyndon Baines Johnson appointed Thurgood Marshall as chief justice of the Supreme Court he was working as the **chief executive**.

# chief legislator

*president's job in the lawmaking process*

**What it is:** the president's role in the legislative process

**How it works:** Although the president doesn't make laws, they do play a role in the lawmaking process. As chief legislator, the president uses their power and influence to propose laws to Congress that align with their agenda. The president can use the bully pulpit and their role as the head of their political party to get public opinion on their side and encourage members of Congress to pass certain laws. Additionally, the president has the power to sign a bill into law or to veto legislation, which gives them ultimate authority on what becomes law.

**How it is used:** The president acted as **chief legislator** this week when they vetoed a law they disagreed with.

# chief of staff

*the head of the president's staff*

**What it is:** the person who leads the president's support staff in the White House

**How it works:** The role of chief of staff is an incredibly important one in the executive branch. This person is one of the president's closest advisers, working to help achieve the president's agenda during their time in office. The chief of staff determines which information to give the president, filtering out unnecessary information while ensuring the president is briefed on important matters. They also help to oversee projects and initiatives of the president and their administration.

**How it is used:** Responsibilities of the White House **chief of staff** include determining who gets access to the president and managing the White House staff on a day-to-day basis.

# chief of state



**What it is:** the role of the president as the ceremonial head of the government

**How it works:** In many countries, the chief of state is a separate role from the political leader of the country. In the United States, however, the president fills both roles. As chief of state, the president acts as the ceremonial head of the nation. This role includes participating in cultural traditions, such as hosting the White House Easter Egg Roll on the front lawn or pardoning a turkey on Thanksgiving. This also includes recognizing the achievements of Americans by receiving them at the White House or honoring them at events throughout the country.

**How it is used:** The president exercised their role as **chief of state** when inviting American Olympic gold medalists to the White House to honor their achievements.

# commander in chief



**What it is:** the president's role as the top commander of the country's armed forces

**How it works:** As commander in chief of the United States Armed Forces, the president is at the top of the chain of command. In this role, the president can control troop movements, especially during times of declared war. The president can determine where troops are stationed and what actions they take. The president is also in charge of military promotions. Additionally, the president has control of the nation's nuclear weapons, which can't be used without their command. Some presidents don't have a military background, so they surround themselves with top generals and admirals to help make decisions.

**How it is used:** When President Harry S. Truman made the decision to drop the atomic bomb on Japan to end World War II, he was acting as **commander in chief**.

# Department of Agriculture



**What it is:** a division of the executive branch focused on policies related to agriculture

**How it works:** The U.S. Department of Agriculture was created in 1862 by President Abraham Lincoln. It's primarily concerned with issues related to agriculture, including food, farming, ranching, forestry, sustainability, trade, and markets. It also helps create and enforce public policy regarding natural resources, rural development, and nutrition. The goals of the department are to help rural communities in the US thrive, while also supporting nutritious agricultural production. The Department of Agriculture consists of twenty-nine agencies and offices across 4,500 locations, with nearly one hundred thousand employees.

**How it is used:** The **Department of Agriculture** oversees the National School Lunch Program, the Food Safety and Inspection Service, and the Rural Housing Service, among many other things.

# Department of Commerce



**What it is:** a division of the executive branch focused on policies related to trade and business

**How it works:** The U.S. Department of Commerce was originally created in 1903 under President Theodore Roosevelt as the U.S. Department of Commerce and Labor. This department focuses on fostering, serving, and promoting US economic development and technological innovation. Its goal is to create conditions for economic growth and opportunities for all communities in the United States. Its work aims to spur economic competition, strengthen American industry, and promote the growth of jobs. This department acts through business policy and through a commitment to advance technological innovation. Made up of thirteen bureaus, this department is the champion of business in the federal government.

**How it is used:** Some of the bureaus that the **Department of Commerce** oversees are the U.S. Census Bureau, the National Oceanic and Atmospheric Administration, and the National Institute of Standards and Technology.

# Department of Defense



**What it is:** a division of the executive branch focused on policies related to the military and national defense

**How it works:** The U.S. Department of Defense was officially created in 1947 under President Harry S. Truman, when the Departments of War, Navy, and Air Force were combined. The largest department in the executive branch, the Department of Defense includes all active-duty members of the United States Coast Guard, Army, Navy, Marine Corps, Air Force, and Space Force, as well as all members of the National Guard. Many civilians are also employed to help the department create policies, manage resources, and assess programs. The department operates out of the Pentagon. The goals of this department are to deter war while protecting the American people and national security.

**How it is used:** The **Department of Defense** receives over half of the annual discretionary spending budget each year.

# Department of Education



**What it is:** a division of the executive branch focused on policies related to education

**How it works:** The U.S. Department of Education was created in 1979 under President Jimmy Carter. It's the primary educational agency of the federal government. It strives to promote excellent schooling for all Americans, aiming to increase the United States' educational competitiveness on a global level. The department provides services for students, including those with disabilities. The department helps share effective teaching practices with teachers and provides data about schools in the United States. It also provides financial aid services for higher education.

**How it is used:** The Federal Student Aid program, which provides federal grants for higher education and other forms of financial aid after individuals complete the FAFSA (Free Application for Federal Student Aid), is provided by the **Department of Education**.

# Department of Energy



**What it is:** a division of the executive branch focused on policies related to types and uses of energy

**How it works:** The U.S. Department of Energy was created in 1977 under President Jimmy Carter. The department focuses on security and safety, scientific excellence, the environment, energy access, economic growth, and global diplomacy and leadership. The department's mission is to tackle the energy, environmental, and nuclear challenges in the US through scientific research and progress. Additionally, the department works to push the United States forward as a leader in energy technologies, while promoting science and engineering as key drivers of economic growth.

**How it is used:** The **Department of Energy** prides itself on having direct associations with more than 115 Nobel Prize laureates in scientific fields, demonstrating a long-standing commitment to scientific excellence.

# Department of Health and Human Services



**What it is:** a division of the executive branch focused on policies related to public health and the general welfare of American citizens

**How it works:** The U.S. Department of Health and Human Services was originally established in 1953 under President Dwight D. Eisenhower as the

Department of Health, Education, and Welfare. The mission of the department is to promote health and wellness for all Americans. It strives to do this by providing health services for Americans while also conducting research in the fields of medicine, social sciences, and public health. Major agencies within the department include the Centers for Disease Control and Prevention, the Food and Drug Administration, and the National Institutes of Health.

**How it is used:** Through the Centers for Disease Control and Prevention, the **Department of Health and Human Services** manages the Vaccines for Children Program, providing free vaccinations for all children in the country.

## Department of Homeland Security

*enforcer of domestic security policy*

**What it is:** a division of the executive branch focused on policies related to protecting the United States from external threats, such as terrorism

**How it works:** The U.S. Department of Homeland Security was created in 2002 under President George W. Bush as a direct response to the terrorist attacks on September 11, 2001. The department aims to prevent any future attacks on American soil, while assisting citizens as needed during times of crisis, such as natural disasters. Agencies that fall under the leadership of this department include the United States Coast Guard, the Federal Emergency Management Agency, the U.S. Immigration and Customs Enforcement, and the United States Secret Service.

**How it is used:** The **Department of Homeland Security** focuses on a wide range of issues, including protecting Americans from cybersecurity threats and keeping fentanyl out of American communities.

# Department of Housing and Urban Development



**What it is:** a division of the executive branch focused on policies related to home ownership and the development of cities

**How it works:** The U.S. Department of Housing and Urban Development was established in 1965 under President Lyndon B. Johnson. The goals of the department are to increase home ownership and access to affordable housing in the US, while supporting community development. The department helps individuals by providing loans for housing and assistance with the costs of home ownership. Additionally, this department provides grants for community development, initiatives to help people pay for housing, and services for certain groups of people needing further support.

**How it is used:** The Housing Choice Voucher Program, commonly known as Section 8, provides low-income housing as a service through the **Department of Housing and Urban Development**.

# Department of the Interior



**What it is:** a division of the executive branch focused on policies related to natural and cultural resources

**How it works:** The U.S. Department of the Interior was created in 1849 under President Zachary Taylor. Its original purpose was to handle the nation's internal affairs. Today, the department focuses on preserving natural resources and cultural heritage. It employs seventy thousand people across its eleven bureaus and other offices. Divisions of the Department of the Interior include the Bureau of Indian Affairs, the Bureau of Land Management, the National Park Service, and the U.S. Fish and Wildlife Service.

**How it is used:** The **Department of the Interior** manages relationships with the US territories of Guam, American Samoa, and the U.S. Virgin Islands.

# Department of Justice



**What it is:** a division of the executive branch focused on the law

**How it works:** The U.S. Department of Justice was one of the original cabinet departments established during President George Washington's first term in 1789, originally called the Office of the Attorney General. The goals of the department are to maintain rule of law, protect civil rights, and keep Americans safe. The Department of Justice is the law enforcement agency of the federal government. Law enforcement agencies such as the Federal Bureau of Investigation, the Drug Enforcement Administration, and the Bureau of Alcohol, Tobacco, Firearms and Explosives all operate under the Department of Justice. US attorneys who work for this department prosecute federal law violators.

**How it is used:** The **Department of Justice** employs close to ten thousand attorneys to prosecute individuals who violate federal law.

# Department of Labor



**What it is:** a division of the executive branch focused on policies related to the United States' workforce

**How it works:** The U.S. Department of Labor was established in 1913 under President William Howard Taft. The department's goals are to maintain the welfare of America's workers, including those seeking employment and retirees, by improving working conditions and guaranteeing workplace rights and benefits. The department also works to create opportunities for employment. Major agencies under the purview of the Department of Labor include the Bureau of Labor Statistics, the Employee Benefits Security Administration, and the Occupational Safety and Health Administration.

**How it is used:** The Bureau of Labor Statistics in the **Department of Labor** releases a jobs report every month to highlight the increase and decrease of employment in the US.

# Department of State



**What it is:** a division of the executive branch focused on policies related to international relations

**How it works:** One of the first executive departments created, the U.S. Department of State has served an important role in the federal government since 1789. The mission of the department is to help create a positive international environment, while protecting and advancing the security, status, and democratic values of the United States. This department handles issues of foreign policy, including trade, conflict, and strategic deals. The United States' ambassadors work for this department, and the impact of their work can be felt around the world.

**How it is used:** The **Department of State** has six regional bureaus, each focused on developing US foreign policies for specific areas of the world.

# Department of Transportation



**What it is:** a division of the executive branch focused on policies related to infrastructure and transportation

**How it works:** The U.S. Department of Transportation was created in 1966 under President Lyndon B. Johnson. This department's focus is on creating reliable and efficient transportation systems in the United States for all forms of travel, prioritizing safety in travel and systems that can adapt with the future. Agencies that work under the umbrella of the Department of Transportation include the Federal Aviation Administration, the Federal Highway

Administration, the Federal Transit Administration, and the Federal Railroad Administration.

**How it is used:** Under the **Department of Transportation**, the Federal Highway Administration works with state governments to construct and maintain highways across the United States.

# Department of the Treasury

*enforcer of economic policy*

**What it is:** a division of the executive branch focused on economic strategy and law

**How it works:** One of the original cabinet departments established under President George Washington in 1789, the U.S. Department of the Treasury works to promote economic prosperity in the United States. It strives to maintain a healthy economy by enacting policies that allow for stability in the marketplace. The department also works to protect the nation's financial institutions. Additionally, this department collects taxes, pays the United States' bills, manages the nation's public debt, coins and prints money, and prosecutes tax evaders and counterfeiters.

**How it is used:** Agencies that are part of the **Department of the Treasury** include the Internal Revenue Service, the Bureau of Engraving and Printing, and the United States Mint.

# Department of Veterans Affairs

*enforcer of veterans' policies*

**What it is:** a division of the executive branch focused on policies related to veterans

**How it works:** The U.S. Department of Veterans Affairs was established in 1988 under President Ronald Reagan. Prior to this, it was the Veterans Administration and had been operating since 1930. This department's sole purpose is to help those who have served in the military and their families. The department focuses on veterans' healthcare and benefits, as well as national cemeteries where veterans can be buried. Housing assistance, education benefits, and pension information are also available for veterans through this department.

**How it is used:** The National Cemetery Administration is an agency in the **Department of Veterans Affairs** that maintains American military cemeteries in the United States and abroad, providing a final resting place to honor veterans.

# discretionary authority



**What it is:** the power of bureaucratic agencies to make decisions when it comes to implementing laws

**How it works:** After laws pass through Congress and the president, they often lack specific outlines for how the laws should be implemented. Bureaucratic departments and agencies have to decide the best way to carry out the law. This is their discretionary authority. As experts in their field, bureaucrats know how to best execute laws related to their policy area. Discretionary authority gives the bureaucracy more independence and power.

**How it is used:** Although the executive departments have **discretionary authority**, Congress maintains the power of oversight to ensure they don't abuse their power.

# executive agreement



**What it is:** an agreement made by the president with leaders of other nations

**How it works:** The Constitution gives the president the power to make treaties, which require approval from the Senate. Over time, US presidents have learned that making executive agreements with nations works similarly to treaties, but these agreements don't need Senate approval. Essentially working like a pact between two countries, executive agreements allow the president to make deals with other nations with fewer restrictions and more efficiency. These agreements do carry the weight of law, but they can be changed by future presidents.

**How it is used:** An example of an **executive agreement** is the North American Free Trade Agreement, first signed by President George H.W. Bush to create fewer trade restrictions between the US, Mexico, and Canada.

# executive order



**What it is:** an official document issued by the president that carries the weight of law

**How it works:** The president has many powers, but they can't make laws, except in the form of an executive order. Executive orders have the force of law but don't require congressional approval. Traditionally, executive orders were used for administrative duties, but over time, presidents started using them to establish policies and programs. This includes creating rules and instructions for carrying out certain laws. Some well-known executive orders include President Franklin D. Roosevelt's order for Japanese internment during World War II and President Harry S. Truman's order that desegregated the military in 1948. Executive orders are subject to judicial review.

**How it is used:** To date, President Franklin D. Roosevelt issued the most **executive orders** of any president, with 3,726 put into effect.

# executive privilege



**What it is:** the president's power to keep certain conversations confidential

**How it works:** Over the course of a president's time in office, they have an immeasurable number of meetings and conversations. Sometimes, Congress wants to know what happens in these meetings. If the president doesn't want to share this information, they can invoke executive privilege. In order for the president to make the best decisions about government policy and actions, they need their advisers to be candid with them. If an adviser knows that what they say could be shared with Congress or the larger public, they may not speak honestly in these meetings. These candid conversations, though, are essential for effective government.

**How it is used:** The president can't use the power of **executive privilege** during investigations into criminal activity, as established by the Supreme Court case *United States v. Nixon*.

# First Spouse


*the president's spouse*

**What it is:** the spouse of the current president

**How it works:** If a president is married, their spouse is known as the First Spouse. Until this point in time, there have been only First Ladies. Although not a political role, the First Spouse plays an important part in the administration of the president. They're considered to be the host of the White House and are responsible for planning events such as state dinners with foreign dignitaries. The First Spouse also represents the president at ceremonial events. Over time, the role of First Spouse has become more influential, as many spouses have taken up social causes to pursue through their platform.

**How it is used:** Eleanor Roosevelt, through her role as **First Spouse**, advised her husband on major political issues, advocated for social justice, and ran programs that helped Americans during World War II.

# government corporations

*government-owned companies*

**What it is:** companies that are owned and operated by the federal government

**How it works:** Although most businesses in the United States are privately owned, there are some that the government controls. These government corporations exist for a variety of reasons. In some cases, the government is attempting to control a business that would naturally become a monopoly. In others, the government wants to ensure that important things, like infrastructure and public benefits, are effectively taken care of and maintained. Government corporations operate to provide services for Americans and to take care of government goals; they don't operate to make a profit.

**How it is used:** The U.S. Postal Service, National Railroad Passenger Corporation (Amtrak), and the Federal Deposit Insurance Corporation are all examples of **government corporations**.

# Hatch Act

*no politics in government jobs*

**What it is:** an act that restricts the political activity of certain government officials

**How it works:** The Hatch Act of 1939 was passed in an effort to create a nonpartisan working environment for government officials in the bureaucracy. With the execution of laws and programs, it's important to remove politics to ensure impartial implementation. This act also keeps employees from being forced to participate in political activities through their government job. Certain activities are banned for most federal employees while at work, including working for a political campaign, soliciting campaign donations, and using government resources for political reasons.

**How it is used:** Although the **Hatch Act** restricts the political activity of government employees while on duty or in a federal facility, it doesn't restrict their actions while off duty.

# honeymoon period

*popular president*

**What it is:** a period of great popularity for a new president

**How it works:** When new presidents come into office, most are said to enjoy a honeymoon period. This is a time when public opinion is optimistic about their administration. People are hopeful about the new leadership and are typically supportive of the president. This can give the new president momentum to make changes and pursue their agenda. Honeymoon periods don't usually last long, with most coming to an end after a couple of months. New presidents capitalize on this period by trying to keep a positive public image and high approval ratings.

**How it is used:** President Dwight D. Eisenhower was an exceedingly popular president, with a **honeymoon period** lasting forty-one months during his first term in office.

# impoundment

*stopping government funds*

**What it is:** the president withholding government funds that have already been approved by Congress

**How it works:** Congress approves the spending of all government agencies, while the president administers the funds. An impoundment is when the president delays or withholds these funds. The president might do this to save money or because they don't support the program the funds are going to. In 1974, Congress passed the Impoundment Control Act, which limits this presidential power by allowing only temporary impoundments through either deferrals or rescissions. A deferral limits the funding for the fiscal year, while a rescission is a more permanent measure that must be approved by Congress.

**How it is used:** The Supreme Court ruled that **impoundments** by the president are unconstitutional in the case *Train v. City of New York*, although there are still controversies surrounding the issue.

# independent executive agency



**What it is:** a federal government agency that has independent authority over a certain policy area

**How it works:** Although independent executive agencies work to enforce laws, they're separate from the executive departments. The purview of these agencies tend to be highly specialized, as they handle critical tasks related to important issues in the US. Although the agencies are separate from the cabinet, the president still appoints their leaders. Presidential control of independent executive agencies is limited, as removing the directors requires justifiable cause. Often, these agencies are insulated from party politics.

**How it is used:** The Central Intelligence Agency and the Environmental Protection Agency are **independent executive agencies**.

# independent regulatory commission



**What it is:** a specific group of the federal government that issues regulations on certain businesses or economic activities

**How it works:** Independent regulatory commissions are agencies free from executive control and can't be easily dissolved or changed. Their leaders are appointed by the president and approved by the Senate, but they can't be removed without just cause. They serve for a fixed term, furthering their independence from the federal government and politics. These agencies protect public interests by establishing and enforcing regulations. The aim of regulatory commissions is to ensure fair competition in business, safety for Americans, and stability of the economy. These commissions cover broad areas like finance, transportation, and communications.

**How it is used:** The Federal Communications Commission and the Federal Trade Commission are **independent regulatory commissions**.

# iron triangle



**What it is:** the relationship between an interest group, congressional committee, and federal agency

**How it works:** When making policies, many groups come together to collaborate on the issues. One such network is called an iron triangle, or a subgovernment. This mutually beneficial relationship exists between interest groups advocating for certain issues, congressional committees that write the law, and government agencies that implement the policy. For example, special interest groups support the reelection campaigns of congressional committee members, who then pass laws and increase the budgets of federal agencies that implement policies benefiting those interest groups. Although these groups can make things more efficient, they don't always serve the interests of the public.

**How it is used:** An **iron triangle** exists between the AARP, the U.S. Senate Special Committee on Aging, and the Social Security Administration.

# issue network



**What it is:** the complicated connection between various groups interested in the lawmaking process

**How it works:** An issue network is the collection of people and ideas that come together to advocate for policy. This can involve interest groups, think tanks, government officials, representatives from the private sector, and other groups who join forces to champion certain public policy issues. Unlike a traditional special interest group or an iron triangle, issue networks are more fluid and centered around shared interests, bringing together diverse perspectives and opinions. With the Internet and social media, issue networks have become more successful.

**How it is used:** An **issue network** exists among journalists, nonprofit groups, citizens, researchers, and businesses to advocate for government transparency.

# Joint Chiefs of Staff



**What it is:** a group of high-ranking military officials who advise the president

**How it works:** The president is commander in chief of the United States Armed Forces but doesn't necessarily have extensive military experience. The president needs advisers who are experts in defense and military strategy. The Joint Chiefs of Staff are these experts. This group consists of the heads of each branch of the military, who are appointed by the president and confirmed by the Senate. Together, they advise the president, secretary of defense, and National Security Council on matters concerning the military. The Joint Chiefs of Staff don't have any authority to command troops from this position.

**How it is used:** The **Joint Chiefs of Staff** met with the president to discuss ongoing military efforts to combat terrorism.

# lame duck president



**What it is:** the period of time after the presidential election and before the inauguration of a new president

**How it works:** A president is considered a lame duck when they're nearing the end of their term and won't be serving another. This can happen because they lost their reelection, chose not to run for a second term, or met the term limits and can't run again. During this time, the president can be less effective because members of Congress, and the people, are more focused on the incoming president and their promises for change. Alternatively, some presidents use this time to take bold measures and pass more extreme policies since they have nothing to lose.

**How it is used:** During his **lame duck** period, President Bill Clinton passed 140 pardons and commuted thirty-six sentences, some of which caused significant controversy.

# line-item veto



**What it is:** the act of a president rejecting a line or section of a bill instead of the whole thing

**How it works:** The line-item veto allows for an executive to veto only a portion of a bill instead of its entirety. Although this concept would allow for more legislation to be passed, it was ruled as a violation of separation of powers and considered unconstitutional by the Supreme Court in the 1998 case *Clinton v. City of New York*. Some governors have this power, but if the president doesn't like a section of a bill, they must veto the entire bill.

**How it is used:** The **line-item veto** was ruled unconstitutional because it gave the president more lawmaking powers than the Constitution permits.

# merit-based system



**What it is:** the system where government employees earn their jobs through education, experience, and competition

**How it works:** Throughout history, government employees were often hired not because of their knowledge and skill but because of their connections to people in power. In 1883, the Pendleton Act was passed in an effort to stop this practice. Jobs were to be awarded on a merit-based system, where individuals would have to take competitive exams. Today, people must demonstrate competence in the field they're entering. The Pendleton Act also protects government employees from being fired for political reasons, allowing people to keep their jobs because of their performance and not their political affiliation.

**How it is used:** In the United States today, around 85 percent of federal jobs are filled through the **merit-based system**.

# national debt



**What it is:** the money that the government owes after borrowing money

**How it works:** Currently, the federal budget practices deficit spending, meaning that the government spends more than it brings in. To make up for this overspending, the government borrows money from the public by issuing Treasury bills and savings bonds. The amount that the government has borrowed adds up to the national debt. This staggering number continues to rise each year, as deficits continue to occur. The government does not have to pay it off all at once, but it does have to pay interest every year, which makes up a significant portion of the federal budget.

**How it is used:** In 2025, the **national debt** exceeded $38 trillion.

# National Security Council



**What it is:** a group of individuals in the federal government who advise the president on national security issues and foreign affairs

**How it works:** The National Security Council is made up of the vice president, the secretary of state, the secretary of defense, the secretary of the treasury, and the secretary of energy, as well as the Joint Chiefs of Staff and the director of national intelligence. Other individuals, such as the national security adviser and the chief of staff, also serve on the council. This council's primary duty is to advise the president on policy and actions related to national security, foreign affairs, and military policies. The advisers work together from their respective departments to align the goals of the president and enact policy.

**How it is used:** The **National Security Council** was created in 1947 as a way to bring together different executive departments and to coordinate international and military policy.

# naturalization



**What it is:** the process for becoming a legal citizen of a country

**How it works:** When people immigrate to the United States, there are certain processes they must go through. If they have plans to stay in the US and want the privileges that come with being a citizen, like the right to vote and receive government services, they must naturalize. This is a lengthy process that includes background checks, paperwork, and determining eligibility. Additionally, one must also take the naturalization exam, which asks questions about US history, government, and geography. If they pass, they must take an Oath of Allegiance at a naturalization ceremony.

**How it is used:** In fiscal year 2024, over 818,000 people went through the **naturalization** process.

# pocket veto



**What it is:** the president's power to veto a bill without officially issuing a veto

**How it works:** When a bill comes to the president's desk, they can sign it into law or veto it and send it back to Congress. The president can veto by officially rejecting it or using a pocket veto. With a pocket veto, the president simply lets the bill sit on their desk. If Congress adjourns within ten days of the bill arriving to the president, the bill is automatically vetoed. If Congress doesn't adjourn, the bill automatically becomes law. Because of this, Congress doesn't typically send important legislation to the president's desk within ten days of adjournment.

**How it is used:** The **pocket veto** is a way for the president to reject a bill without fear of Congress overriding it, since they won't be in session to receive it.

# political patronage



**What it is:** employing close friends or loyal party members once in power

**How it works:** Throughout history, many presidents have practiced political patronage. Also called the spoils system, political patronage supports the idea that the victors receive the spoils of war. If someone wins an election, they take advantage and give loyal party members jobs in the government, regardless of their qualifications. Often, competent employees would be fired so these jobs could be filled. After President James A. Garfield was assassinated by a disgruntled party member who was denied a job, Congress passed the Pendleton Act, creating the standard for merit-based hiring in the federal government.

**How it is used:** An advocate of **political patronage**, President Andrew Jackson had more than nine hundred people removed from their jobs so he could replace them with people loyal to him.

# president



**What it is:** the leader of a country's executive branch

**How it works:** The president is the head of the branch of government that executes, or enforces, the laws. In the United States, the president must be at least thirty-five years old, a US citizen from birth, and a resident of the United States for at least fourteen years. The president is indirectly elected by the people through the Electoral College every four years. Presidents can serve only two terms, per the 22nd Amendment to the Constitution. The president serves many roles, including chief executive, chief diplomat, commander in chief, chief of state, and chief legislator (all of which are defined in this chapter).

**How it is used:** President Franklin D. Roosevelt was elected to four terms as **president** through the Great Depression and World War II, leading Congress to propose the 22nd Amendment, limiting the terms of future presidents.

# Presidential Succession Act



**What it is:** the act that establishes the line of succession to the presidency

**How it works:** Throughout US history, eight presidents have died in office—four died from natural causes and four have been assassinated. Additionally, one president has resigned. A plan was needed for who takes over in these situations. In 1947, the Presidential Succession Act was created, establishing a line of succession. If the president can no longer serve, the vice president takes over, followed by the Speaker of the House, president pro tempore of the Senate, and then the cabinet secretaries in the order their cabinet departments were created. To date, the vice president is the only one in the line of succession to have taken over.

**How it is used:** President Harry S. Truman believed it was more democratic to have the Speaker of the House second in the **Presidential Succession Act**, ahead of the president pro tempore of the Senate, since the people elect members of Congress.

# press secretary



**What it is:** the president's chosen person to speak to the press on matters of national importance

**How it works:** In a republic, the connection between the government and the people comes most often from the media, or the press. The press secretary is the official media spokesperson for the executive branch. This person hosts daily briefings to keep the press informed and answer questions. As the person interacting with the media on a daily basis, the press secretary also plays an important role in deciding how to present information to the public. This role also includes working with reporters and news agencies to shape the president's message.

**How it is used:** The White House **press secretary** hosted a press conference to discuss the president's response to a major issue.

# recess appointment



**What it is:** the president's power to employ certain government positions when the Senate is in recess

**How it works:** The president has the power to appoint many government officials with the approval of the Senate. Article 2 of the Constitution states that if a vacancy occurs in any presidential-appointed position when the Senate isn't in session, then the president can fill the position without Senate approval. Recess appointments can last until the end of the Senate's next session. As such, recess appointments can potentially last for almost two years. The Supreme Court has ruled that in order for a recess appointment to be valid, the Senate's recess must be at least ten days.

**How it is used:** Presidents Bill Clinton and George W. Bush both used the **recess appointment** power to fill government positions, with Clinton using it 139 times and Bush 171 times.

# rulemaking power



**What it is:** the bureaucracy's authority to make rules about the implementation of laws

**How it works:** Similar to the bureaucracy's discretionary authority, the bureaucracy's rulemaking power comes from the lack of detail in laws once they are passed by Congress and the president. Rulemaking power allows the bureaucracy to set regulations and enforce those regulations if individuals, companies, or states violate them. This power is subject to Congress's oversight, but it gives the bureaucracy considerable power. For example, the Environmental Protection Agency sets standards for pollution that all states and corporations must follow.

**How it is used:** The Internal Revenue Service uses its **rulemaking power** to set procedures for the collection of taxes, such as the April 15 filing deadline.

# secretary of state



**What it is:** the leader of the Department of State who serves as the chief foreign policy adviser to the president

**How it works:** Every executive department has a leader called a secretary. These individuals are appointed by the president and confirmed by the Senate. The secretary of state is the head of the Department of State. This individual serves as an adviser to the president regarding foreign policy and international affairs. They serve to execute the foreign policies promoted and created by the president. Whenever there's a situation involving the US and another country, the secretary of state works with the president to resolve the issue.

**How it is used:** Thomas Jefferson resigned from his position as the nation's first **secretary of state** in 1793 after President George Washington remained neutral regarding the French Revolution; Jefferson believed that the United States should have gotten involved.

# State of the Union address



**What it is:** the annual speech given by the president to Congress, where the president gives their view of the nation's major problems and their solutions

**How it works:** The Constitution dictates that the president must address Congress about the state of the union. This address is a time for the president to gather all the members of Congress, Supreme Court justices, and cabinet secretaries to update them on the major issues the US is facing. This is also a time for the president to state how they intend to solve these problems. Typically delivered at the beginning of the year, this speech sets the stage for the president's upcoming legislative agenda.

**How it is used:** The **State of the Union address** is televised so the president's message can reach all Americans.

# tariff



**What it is:** a tax placed on goods being imported into the country

**How it works:** Tariffs are a type of tax that have been around since the beginning of the United States. The goal with most tariffs is to make foreign goods more expensive in an effort to support American businesses. Tariffs can be used for other reasons too, such as encouraging trade deals and attempting to eliminate a certain type of trade. As a type of taxation, Congress has the power to institute tariffs. But because these taxes heavily impact foreign relations, Congress has delegated this power to the president.

**How it is used:** In 1930, President Herbert Hoover implemented the Hawley–Smoot **Tariff** Act, taxing twenty thousand imported goods to help American businesses during the Great Depression.

# veto power



**What it is:** the president's power to deny legislation

**How it works:** One of the major checks the president has on Congress is the ability to veto legislation that has passed through both houses. If a president vetoes a bill, they reject it, and it doesn't become law unless Congress overrides the veto with a two-thirds majority vote in both houses. Because of how difficult it is to override a veto, the simple mention of a possible veto can be enough to sway members of Congress to change a bill more to the president's liking.

**How it is used:** Throughout both his terms, President Grover Cleveland used the **veto power** 584 times.

# vice president



**What it is:** the person who's second-in-command to the president

**How it works:** Originally, the vice president of the United States was the person who came in second in the presidential election. As political parties grew, the complications of this system arose, leading to the passage of the 12th Amendment, which created the system the US uses now. The vice president's only constitutional responsibility, other than being in line for the presidential succession, is to be the president of the Senate. Other than that, the vice president works alongside the president to promote the agenda of their party. It's up to the president to determine how active a role the vice president plays in their administration.

**How it is used:** As **vice president** under Ronald Reagan, George H.W. Bush played a key role in foreign policy during the Cold War.

# War Powers Act



**What it is:** an act that sets specific parameters on the president's war-making powers

**How it works:** Congress has the power to declare war. As commander in chief, the president has the power to move troops around the world. During the Cold War, the president used this power to bring the country into numerous military conflicts, none of which were officially declared as war. Congress, in an effort to limit the president's power, passed the War Powers Resolution of 1973. Now, if the president moves troops, they must tell Congress within forty-eight hours. Unless Congress has approved the move, troops must be brought home within sixty days, with the exception of a thirty-day extension in some cases.

**How it is used:** President Richard Nixon vetoed the **War Powers Act**, but Congress overrode the veto, making it law.

# White House press corps

*journalists at the White House*

**What it is:** a group of reporters whose job is to report on the president and the executive branch

**How it works:** The media is often called the fourth branch of government, as it serves the people by reporting on what the government is doing. A number of media outlets have journalists assigned to the White House press corps. As part of this group, these reporters work in the White House, working closely with the press secretary and gaining access to advisers and members of the president's staff. A small number are selected as part of the press pool and travel with the president on Air Force One, the presidential aircraft.

**How it is used:** Originally the **White House press corps** consisted of only newspaper reporters, but radio reporters were added in the 1940s followed by television reporters in the 1950s.

# Chapter 5

# THE JUDICIAL BRANCH

Article 3 of the Constitution outlines the powers and duties of the judicial branch. Although this section of the Constitution is relatively short compared to the others, the judicial branch plays an integral role in the United States government. Not only does this branch serve as a check on the others by exerting its power of judicial review, but it also is where you'll see the rules of the US justice system defined.

Many people associate the judicial branch with just the Supreme Court, but it's also made up of many lower courts with different jurisdictions and roles in American government. This chapter focuses on the structure of the court system in the United States. Here you will learn about the difference between appellate and original jurisdiction, a prosecutor and defendant, and a felony and misdemeanor. From the makeup of the courts and their powers to the terms you can expect to hear in courtrooms, this chapter covers it all.

# amicus curiae brief



**What it is:** a document submitted by a special interest group to the Supreme Court in an effort to influence a ruling

**How it works:** Interest groups can't directly lobby the Supreme Court. As such, when they aren't the ones arguing a case, interest groups will submit an amicus curiae brief to let the Supreme Court know their stance on an issue in which they have a strong interest. These documents help Supreme Court justices understand the impact of their ruling on the groups' interest and the people they represent. This is one way that interest groups can attempt to influence the Supreme Court. Supreme Court opinions sometimes use the amicus curiae briefs in their arguments, and occasionally the group that filed the brief will present it before the court.

**How it is used:** The American Civil Liberties Union filed an **amicus curiae brief** with the Supreme Court regarding a case about civil rights.

# appellate jurisdiction



**What it is:** the authority of a court to hear cases appealing an earlier ruling

**How it works:** In the American court system, individuals can appeal (challenge) a ruling from an earlier case if they believe an error was made during the original trial. Whenever a party chooses to appeal, their case is brought to an appeals court that has appellate jurisdiction. In these cases, there is no jury, and the judges don't hear from witnesses. Instead, judges hear from the two sides of the original case and ask questions related to the alleged error. When this court rules, it can overturn a sentence or grant a retrial where the errors will be corrected.

**How it is used:** The thirteen US courts of appeals have **appellate jurisdiction**.

# attorney general



**What it is:** the top prosecutor for the federal government and an adviser to the president

**How it works:** The attorney general is appointed by the president and confirmed by the Senate, like all heads of executive departments. The person in this position generally changes with each new president. They serve as an adviser to the president as a member of their cabinet. The attorney general gives the president and their administration advice on legal matters relating to the United States. The attorney general also serves as the chief law enforcement officer for the United States and their office brings charges against individuals who have allegedly broken federal law.

**How it is used:** As the head of the Department of Justice, the **attorney general** brought charges against suspected members of a drug cartel.

# bail



**What it is:** collateral that a defendant provides to leave jail while awaiting trial

**How it works:** After a person is arrested for allegedly committing a crime, they sometimes have the opportunity to put up bail, so that they may be released from jail before their trial starts. The money for bail is collateral and will likely be returned to the defendant if they show up for their court date. A judge determines the amount of bail an individual must provide based on the crime, the likelihood that the defendant will flee, the defendant's connections to the community, and other factors that might influence the trial itself.

**How it is used:** The 8th Amendment protects individuals from excessive **bail**.

# bench trial



**What it is:** a trial where the outcome is determined by a judge

**How it works:** In bench trials, a judge hears the evidence and makes a final decision regarding the outcome of the case. Bench trials are used to help speed up the legal process, as the task of selecting a jury takes time. In cases with more nuanced and technical legal issues, a bench trial might be the preferred method, as a judge may understand the issues better than a jury. To have a bench trial, both parties must waive their right to a trial by jury.

**How it is used:** In 2018, only 12 percent of defendants who went to trial opted for a **bench trial**.

# binding precedent



**What it is:** the courts must accept the decisions of higher courts in similar cases

**How it works:** In the United States, all lower-level courts must follow the rulings made by higher-level courts (appellate courts) when dealing with similar cases. For example, all Supreme Court case decisions bind all other federal courts, meaning that they must rule in the same manner as the Supreme Court. This ensures that there's consistency, stability, and fairness in the legal system. Judges use precedent to guide their decisions, and lawyers use it to argue why a judge should rule a certain way. Sometimes, the Supreme Court overturns precedent, which has a major influence on how the lower courts rule.

**How it is used: Binding precedent** is a major part of the principle of *stare decisis*, meaning "to stand by things decided."

# burden of proof



**What it is:** the government's responsibility to prove guilt in a criminal trial

**How it works:** In a criminal trial, the defendant is innocent until proven guilty, so the burden of proof always falls on the government, or the prosecution. The job of a prosecutor is to bring charges against someone who they have evidence against. It's not the responsibility of that individual to prove their innocence, but it is the responsibility of the prosecution to prove their guilt. To convict in a criminal case, juries must believe beyond a reasonable doubt that someone has committed the crime they're being charged with.

**How it is used:** The founding leaders placed the **burden of proof** on the government as a way to protect individual rights and limit the government from abusing its power.

# capital punishment



**What it is:** the term used to describe the punishment of execution for one's crimes

**How it works:** In the US, capital punishment is a possible outcome for criminal activity in certain cases. At the federal level, the death penalty is legal. Crimes that could result in the death penalty include treason, espionage, murder, and other crimes that result in death. But at the state level, the death penalty depends on the individual state; some states don't have the death penalty, while others do. Most cases that result in capital punishment at the state level involve a murder.

**How it is used:** At present, twenty-seven states in the United States have **capital punishment** as a possible sentence for certain crimes.

# chief justice



**What it is:** the presiding officer of the highest court in the US legal system

**How it works:** The chief justice of the United States is the most senior member of the Supreme Court. Although this individual has more responsibilities than the other justices, they don't have more power. The job of chief justice is to ensure that all proper protocols are followed in the Supreme Court and lower federal courts. In the Constitution, the chief justice is assigned the task of presiding over impeachment trials for government officials. The chief justice also administers the presidential oath of office.

**How it is used:** There have been seventeen **chief justices** of the United States since 1789.

# civil courts



**What it is:** a courtroom that resolves disputes between individuals, organizations, or the government

**How it works:** In civil court, the issues aren't about if someone committed a crime. These courts focus on issues such as contract violations, personal injury lawsuits, property disputes, and matters of civil rights and civil liberties. Civil court trials begin when one party files charges against another party. Often, they're seeking monetary compensation as a way to resolve the issue at hand. Per the 7th Amendment, everyone has the right to a trial by jury in a US civil court.

**How it is used:** When she sued her neighbor over a property boundary dispute, they went to **civil court**.

# common law



**What it is:** regulations about issues that aren't codified but are determined by the US court system over time

**How it works:** Common law refers to laws that aren't created by Congress or the state legislatures. Instead, these laws are created by judges in the judicial branch over time. As judges make rulings on different issues, these rulings serve as a precedent that future judges can look to. The precedents of past cases give judges guidance on how to handle issues when there's no official law to guide them. Common law, also known as case law, allows the courts to hear more issues than just those about breaking the written law.

**How it is used: Common law** cases include issues related to property law, contract law, and constitutional law.

# concurring opinion



**What it is:** opinion of the Supreme Court that concurs with the majority opinion but for different reasons

**How it works:** When the Supreme Court rules on a case, it issues opinions that outline the legal justification of the ruling. Justices who agree with the majority but have different legal arguments sometimes write concurring opinions. In these documents, the justice will provide their legal rationale that supports the ruling of the case. Concurring opinions don't have the same legal standing as the majority opinion. Not all cases have concurring opinions.

**How it is used:** In the 1973 Supreme Court case of *Roe v. Wade*, Justice William Douglas issued a **concurring opinion** that argued a woman's right to have an abortion was connected to unenumerated rights in the 9th Amendment.

# criminal courts



**What it is:** courtrooms that hold trials determining the guilt of alleged criminals

**How it works:** Criminal courts handle cases in which people are being put on trial for suspected criminal activity. These courts exist at both the state and federal level, as there are different laws for each. These courts handle misdemeanor and felony-level crimes. In a criminal courtroom, prosecutors who have filed charges against the defendant present evidence and have witnesses testify to try and prove the defendant's guilt. If someone is found guilty by a jury in a criminal case, they face penalties such as fines, time in prison, or, in some cases, the death penalty.

**How it is used:** The 1995 murder trial of O.J. Simpson is a famous example of a **criminal court** proceeding.

# defendant



**What it is:** the person whom charges have been brought against in a courtroom

**How it works:** In criminal and civil courts, the person who's being charged is known as the defendant. In criminal cases, the defendant has been charged with breaking the law. In civil cases, the defendant is the person being sued. In both types of courts, the defendant must defend themselves by poking holes in the prosecution's arguments and evidence against them; they don't have to prove their innocence. It's up to a judge or jury, depending on the case, to determine whether the defendant is found guilty.

**How it is used:** The **defendant** testified in court to provide their alibi and disprove the prosecution's claims against them.

# dissenting opinion



**What it is:** opinion of the Supreme Court that dissents from the majority opinion

**How it works:** When the Supreme Court rules on a case, it issues opinions that outline the legal justification of the ruling. Justices who didn't vote with the majority sometimes issue dissenting opinions. In these documents, the justice will write about why they don't agree with the majority and how they interpreted the law in question. Although these opinions don't have any legal standing, they're important because they provide insight into the legal process of the Supreme Court and can be referenced for courts facing similar decisions.

**How it is used:** In the 1896 Supreme Court case *Plessy v. Ferguson*, which established the principle of "separate but equal" facilities and condoned segregation, Justice John Marshall Harlan wrote a famous **dissenting opinion** where he argued that the government should not have the authority to legally separate races.

# fair and speedy trial



**What it is:** the constitutional requirement of the justice system to provide a fair and relatively quick trial to all defendants

**How it works:** The 6th Amendment to the Constitution guarantees that all citizens have a fair and speedy trial as a way to ensure that the government doesn't abuse its power. A fair trial is one where the defendant has access to an attorney, can confront witnesses, and has a trial by jury. The guarantee of a speedy trial is important as it requires the government to act and ensures that the accused aren't in jail for an indefinite amount of time. Both of these tenants of the justice system act as a way to protect the rights of the accused.

**How it is used:** The government can't take away an individual's right to a **fair and speedy trial**, even if the crime was particularly heinous.

# felony



**What it is:** a legal misdeed that's serious in nature and has a harsher penalty

**How it works:** In the United States, there are different levels of crimes. A felony is seen as a more consequential crime. Many violent crimes are considered felonies. Some felonies are related to property, while others are related to drugs, money, or lying under oath. Felonies face a punishment of imprisonment for more than one year. In serious cases, the punishment might be the death penalty. Examples of felony-level crimes include murder, burglary, rape, arson, drug trafficking, and aggravated assault.

**How it is used:** A **felony** conviction stays on a person's permanent criminal record.

# grand jury



**What it is:** a group of individuals who rule on indicting a person based on evidence

**How it works:** With certain crimes, before an arrest is made and charges are brought against an individual, the prosecution convenes a grand jury. A grand jury reviews the prosecution's evidence to decide whether there is enough reason to believe a crime was committed and whether the defendant should be put on trial. If the grand jury votes that there is enough evidence, they'll issue an indictment, which formally brings charges against the defendant. Grand juries take place for all federal felonies and other more serious crimes. Grand juries exist at both the federal and state level.

**How it is used:** A **grand jury** usually has between sixteen and twenty-three members and meets a few times each month.

# injunction



**What it is:** a court order for a person to do something or to stop doing something

**How it works:** Injunctions are a tool of the civil courts and offer equitable relief in situations where money alone would not be enough justice. In these cases, the court can make an individual or a group do or stop doing something. Injunctions can result in issuing restraining orders to prevent harassment, temporarily blocking legislation or executive actions, or ordering a violator to cease operations to protect copyright and patents. Injunctions are used in instances when failing to do so would cause irreversible harm to one of the people involved.

**How it is used:** An **injunction** was issued against a company that was violating the copyright of another.

# judge



**What it is:** the individual who ensures fair trials for all in a courtroom

**How it works:** Judges play many roles in the courtroom. They preside over trials, making sure that the courtroom is orderly and follows proper procedure. They act as a referee between the two groups navigating the legal system by ruling on evidence. They ensure that defendants have fair trials by interpreting the law in the courtroom and making sure that the rights of the accused aren't violated. They sentence individuals who are convicted of a crime. And in a bench trial, they issue a verdict on someone's guilt.

**How it is used:** State and local **judges** are often elected to office, while federal judges are appointed by the president and confirmed by the Senate.

# judicial activism



**What it is:** a philosophy that judges in the courts use their position to rule on issues and advocate for policy

**How it works:** Courts have the power of judicial review, which allows them to determine the constitutionality of laws and executive actions. Judicial activism is the belief that the courts should use this power to make decisions that advocate for certain policies, essentially making law. Under this belief, the courts are seen as taking an active role in social and civil rights issues. This is a more liberal philosophy and interpretation of the power of the courts. Although it is most often used in reference to the Supreme Court, judicial activism applies to other courts as well, including state supreme courts and lower federal courts.

**How it is used:** Under Chief Justice Earl Warren in the 1950s and 1960s, the Supreme Court used **judicial activism**, ruling on things such as ending segregation and requiring states to provide attorneys for defendants in all cases.

# judicial restraint



**What it is:** a philosophy that judges in the courts shouldn't use their position to make policy

**How it works:** Judicial restraint supports the idea that the courts, particularly the Supreme Court, should interpret the issues in front of them as closely as possible to the founding leaders' original intent. Under this philosophy, judges sometimes default to the legislature, as the law should represent the will of the people. Judges are still interpreting the law, but they try to do so without inserting their own opinions into their rulings, sticking strictly to what the Constitution or previous court rulings say.

**How it is used:** An example of **judicial restraint** can be found in the 1919 Supreme Court case *Schenck v. United States,* when the court ruled to uphold the Espionage Act even though it limited free speech, thereby deferring to Congress.

# judicial review



**What it is:** the power of the courts to determine whether a law or executive action is constitutional

**How it works:** In 1803, the Supreme Court case *Marbury v. Madison* established the power of judicial review for the Supreme Court. This power gives the judicial branch a much-needed check on the powers of Congress and the president. Using this power, the Supreme Court and other federal courts can review laws made by Congress and actions by the president to determine whether both branches are following the Constitution. If the courts rule something as unconstitutional, then the law is void or the executive action must stop.

**How it is used:** A famous example of the Supreme Court exercising **judicial review** is in the 1954 *Brown v. Board of Education* case where the court ruled that state laws requiring segregation in public schools was unconstitutional.

# legal arbitration



**What it is:** when there's a resolution outside of court regarding noncriminal legal issues

**How it works:** Sometimes, people don't want to go to court for legal issues but still want a resolution. In these cases, arbitration helps. Legal arbitration is when a nonbiased third party mediates issues between parties that cannot resolve their dispute themselves. The arbitrator, or panel of arbitrators, makes a binding decision regarding the issue. This is a way for both parties to avoid the extensive legal fees, time, and energy that go into a court trial.

**How it is used:** An example of **legal arbitration** is if an employee and a company settle a dispute over wrongful termination outside of court by using an arbitrator.

# liberal constructionist



**What it is:** the philosophy of interpreting the Constitution as a living, breathing document that changes with the times

**How it works:** Liberal constructionists are judges who hold the philosophy that the Constitution is a document that is meant to be interpreted differently as time progresses. They believe that it's hard to know the founding leaders' original intent, particularly because the language of the Constitution is vague, so the Constitution should be widely interpreted. Judges with this viewpoint think the founders' underlying purpose was more in framing the Constitution than in the specific words they wrote. This allows judges to apply the Constitution to modern-day issues without being constrained by eighteenth-century thinking.

**How it is used:** While the Constitution is silent on an individual's right to privacy, **liberal constructionists** interpret multiple amendments to include this right and will make rulings that protect it, like in the case *Griswold v. Connecticut*, which established that states could not infringe on a married couple's private choice to use contraceptives.

# majority opinion



**What it is:** the judgment of the Supreme Court that represents the actual ruling on the case

**How it works:** When the Supreme Court rules on a case, it issues opinions that outline the legal justification of the ruling. The majority opinion is often called the opinion of the court because it's the official ruling. This is where those in the majority issue their ruling and detail the legal reasoning behind it. Majority opinions serve as precedent for future decisions of the courts and carry the weight of law. What the court rules is the final stance on the issue, as the Supreme Court is the highest court in the United States.

**How it is used:** The **majority opinion** is typically written by one justice, who is selected either by the chief justice if they're in the majority or by the most senior member of the majority.

# misdemeanor

*lower-level crime*

**What it is:** a less serious criminal offense

**How it works:** A misdemeanor is a crime that's less serious than a felony. Typically, an individual would serve less than twelve months in prison for a misdemeanor, depending on the offense. Other common punishments for misdemeanors are community service, fines, and probation. There are different classifications of misdemeanors in each state and at the federal level. Some misdemeanors include simple assault, disorderly conduct, trespassing, vandalism, petty theft, driving under the influence, and reckless driving.

**How it is used:** Some **misdemeanors** can be removed from a person's permanent criminal record through a process called expungement.

# original jurisdiction

*first level of court*

**What it is:** the level of court where a case is first heard

**How it works:** In the federal justice system, trials are first conducted in original jurisdiction courtrooms. In criminal cases, this is where evidence is provided and witnesses testify in an effort to convict someone of a crime. In civil cases, this is where a legal decision is first made. Article 3 of the Constitution outlines the Supreme Court's judicial power, including its ability to hear disputes between two or more states, cases involving ambassadors, and cases between a state and the federal government, for the first time.

**How it is used:** About 1 percent of the Supreme Court's caseload is for **original jurisdiction** cases.

# parole

*release of a prisoner*

**What it is:** the release of a prisoner before their time is fully served

**How it works:** In the US justice system, prisoners can be granted parole. This can be for a short time for a special purpose, such as a funeral of a loved one, called discretionary parole. Parole can also be mandatory. In some cases, prisoners who exhibit good behavior in prison and whose release would not jeopardize the welfare of the public can be granted mandatory parole. Each case is heard before a board, who then determines whether to grant parole to the individual. If granted parole, they serve the remainder of their sentence outside of the prison, checking in regularly with a parole officer.

**How it is used:** At a **parole** hearing, the person in prison gives their side of the story and provides reasons for why they believe they should be granted parole.

# per curiam opinion

*by-the-court decision*

**What it is:** a decision of the courts that doesn't have an oral argument

**How it works:** Appellate courts typically have oral arguments before they make rulings on cases. In the instance of a per curiam opinion, the court doesn't have oral arguments but instead issues a ruling based on the initial reading of the case. The decision is issued in the name of the entire court and doesn't have a specified author. These opinions are typically used on less controversial, more straightforward cases to help with the court's caseload.

**How it is used:** In the Supreme Court case *Bush v. Gore*, which essentially determined the 2000 presidential election, the Supreme Court issued a **per curiam opinion**.

# petitioner

*person who starts a case*

**What it is:** the individual who files a lawsuit with the court

**How it works:** The term *petitioner* is used in a variety of court proceedings in the United States. Essentially, a petitioner is anyone who files a petition with the courts, and the term is most often used in appeals. In an appeal, the party who lost in the original jurisdiction court asks the appeals court to review their case. These individuals petition, or ask, the court to look over the trial proceedings and subsequent ruling to determine whether legal errors were made.

**How it is used:** The **petitioner** in *Brown v. Board of Education of Topeka* was Oliver Brown, who filed a lawsuit after his daughter Linda Brown was denied admission to an all-white school in Topeka, Kansas.

# plaintiff

*the person filing a lawsuit in civil cases*

**What it is:** the individual who brings charges against someone in a civil case

**How it works:** In civil cases, the individual who starts the lawsuit is known as the plaintiff. In these cases, the plaintiff files a complaint against the defendant. Plaintiffs are seeking a legal remedy for an issue that can't be resolved outside of the court. Oftentimes, they're looking for monetary compensation in the form of damages or for an injunction from the court to stop an action of the defendant's. In civil cases, the plaintiff bears the burden of proof and must prove the claims made against the defendant.

**How it is used:** The **plaintiff** accused the defendant of violating a contract by not providing services agreed upon after being paid.

# plea bargain



**What it is:** when a defendant pleads guilty or no contest to a crime to get concessions from the prosecutor

**How it works:** In some cases, criminal defendants are offered an opportunity to admit to committing the crime in question in exchange for a lesser sentence or some other type of concession. Plea bargains can happen when the prosecution doesn't want to go to trial and has abundant evidence against the defendant. This legal strategy allows the prosecution to avoid the high costs of trials and still seek justice. Plea bargains also allow the defendant an opportunity to negotiate for a lesser sentence.

**How it is used: Plea bargains** make the justice system more efficient but can sometimes be controversial, as there's the potential for innocent defendants to feel pressured to plead guilty.

# preponderance of evidence



**What it is:** the belief that someone most likely committed a certain act

**How it works:** Civil cases require less burden of proof than criminal cases. Criminal cases require juries to believe beyond a reasonable doubt that someone committed a crime before they can issue a guilty verdict. In civil cases, juries need to believe that there's a preponderance of evidence, meaning that the person more likely than not committed the act the plaintiff is accusing them of. If a jury thinks the person is guilty, even if the jurors have doubts, the jury can find them guilty in civil cases.

**How it is used:** When the Smiths sued Bobby for injuries from a car accident, the jury found a **preponderance of evidence** that Bobby was responsible for the crash.

# probation



**What it is:** an alternative to prison time where an individual is supervised in the real world to prevent further criminal activity

**How it works:** One possible punishment for certain lower-level crimes is probation. Probation typically requires individuals to check in with a probation officer regularly and submit to drug testing. These individuals might also have to pay fines depending on the conditions of their probation. Probation allows individuals to face consequences for illegal activities while continuing their lives outside of prison. Often, repeated violations of probation lead to prison sentences. Probation specifics depend on each individual case and can vary from individual to individual.

**How it is used:** Instead of serving jail time for his misdemeanor, he was sentenced to **probation**.

# prosecution



**What it is:** lawyers who file charges for criminal activity and try cases on behalf of the government

**How it works:** In a criminal trial, the prosecution is accusing the defendant of committing a crime. The burden of proof lies with the prosecution, who is acting on behalf of the government to serve justice to those who have broken the law. In order to convict someone, the prosecution must prove beyond a reasonable doubt that the person committed the crime. To do this, they work closely with law enforcement to gather evidence and witness testimonies to prove their points.

**How it is used:** The **prosecution** charged them with murder in the first degree, working with the local sheriff's office to compile evidence.

# respondent



**What it is:** the person or party who responds to legal charges filed against them

**How it works:** In civil cases, the plaintiff files charges against another. This person is known as the respondent, and they must respond to the legal action being taken against them. Essentially, a respondent is the civil case equivalent to a defendant. This term is also used when referencing the two sides of an appellate case. In those cases, the person who is challenging the ruling is a petitioner, and the respondent is defending the ruling of the earlier case. In all cases, the respondent is defending themselves against the charges being brought forth.

**How it is used:** In the Supreme Court case *Brown v. Board of Education of Topeka,* the **respondent** was the Board of Education of Topeka, Kansas, which was seeking to uphold the segregation of schools in its city.

# rule of four



**What it is:** process in the Supreme Court where four justices must agree to bring a case to the court

**How it works:** For appellate cases in the Supreme Court, the justices get to decide whether they'll hear the case. With the rule of four, this means only four of the nine Supreme Court justices need to agree that a case be brought before the court. The rule of four, rather than a simple majority, allows for the minority's voice to not be ignored. This is important to the founding principle of majority rule with minority rights; even if the majority determines the opinion, the minority can bring a case forth.

**How it is used:** The Supreme Court's **rule of four** is not in the Constitution, but is an unwritten, internal practice decided by the justices.

# senatorial courtesy



**What it is:** the informal custom of giving home-state senators major influence over lower-court appointments in their state

**How it works:** The president has the power of appointment for all federal judicial positions, but the Senate must confirm them. With senatorial courtesy, senators will defer to the opinions of the senators who represent the state the appointment is from. If a senator doesn't approve of the appointment in their state, the other senators will deny the appointment as a courtesy. If the home-state senator does approve, then the appointment will be approved. As such, the president looks to the senators of the state where the judge will be presiding for guidance with appointments.

**How it is used: Senatorial courtesy** isn't an official rule of the Senate, but it has been practiced as an unwritten political custom since the beginning of American government.

# solicitor general



**What it is:** a position below the attorney general and deputy attorney general in the Department of Justice

**How it works:** The solicitor general plays an important role in how the US judicial system works. The solicitor general's main job is to argue cases before the Supreme Court on behalf of the United States government. They also argue before other appellate courts. Additionally, the solicitor general determines which cases to appeal and what the legal arguments will be in those cases.

**How it is used:** Elena Kagan, a current associate justice on the Supreme Court, served as the forty-fifth **solicitor general** from 2009–2010.

# statutory law



**What it is:** the laws created by the legislative branch and used by the courts

**How it works:** Statutory law refers to laws that are explicitly written down, or codified. When courts look at statutory law, they're looking at laws created by the legislature. Courts then use these statutes to determine whether someone has violated the law. In these cases, judges apply the law as it's written and don't rely on previous interpretations to guide them. Statutory law can be changed over time, as legislatures create new laws.

**How it is used: Statutory law** includes major legislation passed by Congress such as the Civil Rights Act of 1964 and the Voting Rights Act of 1965.

# strict constructionist



**What it is:** the philosophy of interpreting the Constitution exactly as the founding leaders intended

**How it works:** Strict constructionists are judges who believe that the interpretation of the Constitution should be focused on the original intent of the founding leaders. These judges believe that laws and federal government power should be limited to what's specifically written in the Constitution. Therefore, strict constructionists don't have broad interpretations of the laws before them and tend to uphold actions of the government, so long as there's not a clear violation of the Constitution.

**How it is used:** Justice Antonin Scalia was seen as a **strict constructionist** during his time on the Supreme Court, due to his commitment to *stare decisis* and the original intent of the framers.

# subpoena



**What it is:** an order from the court for someone to attend a hearing

**How it works:** In the US justice system, individuals can be compelled to testify in cases based on their knowledge. If the person doesn't come willingly, and their testimony is important to the case, a subpoena can be issued. This document forces the individual to come to court or face legal consequences, such as fines or imprisonment. Attorneys can issue subpoenas, as can clerks of the court. People can be subpoenaed to court to provide testimony or documents. Congress also can subpoena individuals to testify in congressional hearings.

**How it is used:** People can challenge a **subpoena** on certain grounds, such as arguing that complying with the subpoena would create an unnecessary burden in their lives.

# Supreme Court

*the court of last resort*

**What it is:** the highest court in the United States legal system

**How it works:** The Supreme Court of the United States was established in article 3 of the Constitution. This court is the highest-ranking court in the United States and is the only court to have both original and appellate jurisdiction, meaning it can hear cases first and review decisions from lower courts. The court also exercises the power of judicial review, which is an important check on the power of the legislative and executive branches. The Supreme Court is the final appeals court in the country, and how this court rules becomes the final say on the case.

**How it is used:** The **Supreme Court** typically rules on about eighty cases each year, although it receives approximately 7,000–8,000 petitions for cases.

# Supreme Court justice



**What it is:** a member of the highest court in the United States legal system

**How it works:** The Supreme Court has a panel of judges, known as justices, who make rulings and issue legal justifications for those rulings. Currently, there are nine justices on the court, with one chief justice and eight associate justices. There are no constitutional requirements to be a justice, but traditionally, all justices have backgrounds in law. Supreme Court justices are appointed by the president and confirmed by the Senate. This is often seen as a way for a president to leave a lasting legacy, as justices serve for life and often share judicial philosophies similar to the president who appoints them.

**How it is used:** The Constitution states that all **Supreme Court justices** and other federal judges serve during "good behavior," meaning life, and can be removed through impeachment.

# treason



**What it is:** the act of fighting against a person's country of allegiance

**How it works:** Treason is defined in article 3 of the Constitution as levying war against the United States or as giving aid or comfort to its enemies. To commit treason, an action must take place; thoughts and attitudes aren't enough to convict for treason. The specific definition of treason is important to limit government power, as the government can't claim that someone is a traitor simply because they have different opinions. The Constitution also states that no person can be convicted of treason unless they confess in open court or two witnesses testify to the same overt act.

**How it is used:** In the United States, there have been thirteen people convicted of **treason**, and three people have been executed for it.

# trial by jury



**What it is:** the principle that every person who stands trial has a group of their peers who determines guilt or innocence

**How it works:** The right to a trial by jury was so important to the founding leaders that they embedded it into the body of the Constitution. By having outcomes of most cases determined by a jury and not a judge, the burden of proof is placed on the government, limiting its power over the judicial process. The government must have enough evidence of wrongdoing to convince a group of people, who aren't legal scholars, that someone committed an illegal act. This protects the rights of the accused and helps ensure a fair trial.

**How it is used:** The right to a **trial by jury** can be found in article 3 of the Constitution and in the 6th Amendment.

# U.S. court of appeals



**What it is:** the federal courts who have appellate jurisdiction

**How it works:** In the US legal system, there are thirteen courts of appeals, often called circuit courts. These courts are the level of courts between the district courts and the Supreme Court. Appellate courts don't hear witness testimony or evidence, but they do hear appeals from lower courts and decide if legal errors were made. They determine if the law was correctly applied in earlier cases. A panel of three judges, instead of a jury, makes a ruling. If someone wishes to appeal a district court ruling, they must do so within their court of appeals.

**How it is used:** Most cases must be heard in a **U.S. court of appeals** before making its way to the Supreme Court.

# U.S. district courts



**What it is:** the courts at the federal level that have original jurisdiction

**How it works:** If someone has committed a federal-level crime, or has a civil case at the national level, their trial will take place in a district court. These courts hear evidence and witness testimony to determine the outcome of a case. Typically, the outcome is decided by a jury. There are ninety-four district courts in the United States. Every state has at least one court, while some states have more than that. Cases can be heard by district judges, who are appointed by the president and confirmed by the Senate, or by magistrate judges, who are appointed by the district judge.

**How it is used:** Individuals who believe an error occurred in their **U.S. district court** trial can appeal their case to a circuit court.

# writ of certiorari



**What it is:** a formal order from the Supreme Court for lower courts to send up the information of a proceeding

**How it works:** The Supreme Court determines which cases it hears. When deciding, it looks at a number of factors, including how widespread and impactful the issue is, if it's political in nature, and if it's a newer issue or one that has had time to percolate in society. If the court decides to hear a case, it will issue a writ of certiorari, also called a granting cert. This is a notice given to the lower courts that previously heard the case to send the Supreme Court all the documents they have on this case.

**How it is used:** On average, the Supreme Court issues a **writ of certiorari** in 100–150 of the 7,000 cases appealed to it each year.

# Chapter 6

# POLITICAL PARTICIPATION

The United States government was created for citizens to play an active role. The founding leaders created a republic with the people as the source of power for government officials. To fulfill this duty, people must participate in the political systems that surround them. Political participation encompasses all the ways people can be active citizens and contribute to maintaining the republic created by their ancestors.

Although voting is the number one way to be an active citizen, there are other ways to be a political participant. This chapter discusses the history of voting rights in the United States and the multitude of ways that people can engage with their government. It does a deep dive into the voting process, elections, and political parties to help make sure you understand the crucial role you play in the American government.

# 15th Amendment



**What it is:** the amendment that granted voting rights to African-American men

**How it works:** After the Civil War, during the Reconstruction era, three amendments were passed that served to lift the status of newly freed African Americans. The 15th Amendment focused on enfranchisement (voting rights). With the 15th Amendment, states couldn't deny any man the right to vote due to his race or previous condition of servitude. During the Reconstruction era, African-American men (women still couldn't vote in many states) voted in large numbers and served in office. After the era ended, however, many states passed voter qualification laws that severely restricted African Americans from voting.

**How it is used:** The **15th Amendment** opened up democracy and voting rights for many people in America, although it took many years before it became the norm.

# 19th Amendment



**What it is:** the amendment that universally gave women the right to vote

**How it works:** In 1920, the 19th Amendment to the Constitution was ratified, granting women across the country the right to vote in all local, state, and federal elections. Thousands of women fought for this right for many years leading up to the amendment. Some states granted women the right to vote much earlier; women have been able to vote in Wyoming since it was a territory in 1869. But it was not a nationwide right until 1920. The 19th Amendment ensured that women could not be denied the right to vote because of their sex in any state. This opened up democracy and helped move forward the issue of equality for women.

**How it is used:** The **19th Amendment** was first proposed in Congress in 1878, but it didn't pass until 1919 and took until 1920 to be ratified by the states.

# 26th Amendment



**What it is:** the amendment that lowered the voting age from twenty-one to eighteen

**How it works:** In 1971, the 26th Amendment was passed, lowering the voting age to eighteen. The movement for this amendment stemmed from the Vietnam War. During this tumultuous time in American history, many young men were being drafted at the age of eighteen to fight in the war. Many of these young men felt it was unfair that they were old enough to be drafted but had no say in their government's leadership. The 26th Amendment aimed to fix this concern by lowering the legal voting age from twenty-one to eighteen.

**How it is used:** A popular campaign slogan for the **26th Amendment** was "old enough to fight, old enough to vote."

# absentee ballot

*mail-in voting*

**What it is:** a ballot a voter can submit in advance of Election Day, rather than voting in person at a polling place

**How it works:** Absentee ballots serve to increase voter turnout in elections by allowing people to vote in advance of Election Day, often by mail. This is an especially useful tool for people who are unable to vote in person at their polling place. Each state determines the rules and parameters surrounding absentee voting. Some states send mail-in ballots to all voters regardless of need and conduct all elections through these ballots. Other states may require people to complete an absentee ballot request, with some states requiring a valid excuse for the request, such as being away from the county on Election Day.

**How it is used:** Many college students request **absentee ballots** to be able to vote in elections while away at school.

# ballot



**What it is:** the medium used to cast a vote in an election

**How it works:** Ballots are the tool used to allow people to vote. For many years in the United States, ballots were unsecure and subject to tampering and fraud, but reforms have been put in place to change this. Today, the government ensures that each person has a secret ballot, meaning that the voter casts their vote in private. The vote is counted, but the voter remains anonymous. The ballot method is determined by local and state governments as one of their reserved powers. Some states still use paper ballots, while many others have shifted to electronic voting.

**How it is used:** The secret **ballot** is also known as the Australian ballot, as Australia was the first country to use this method of voting.

# campaign finance laws



**What it is:** legislation determining the limitations on spending and raising money in campaigns

**How it works:** Elections in the United States are expensive for candidates. Over time, laws about how candidates acquire and spend money were implemented. Today, individuals can donate up to $7,000 to a candidate. Candidates for president and Congress can spend their own money on their campaigns with no upward limit. But they must report all campaign funds to the Federal Election Commission. There are other campaign finance laws specific to different groups, such as political action committees and super PACs. You can find more information about these laws throughout this chapter.

**How it is used: Campaign finance laws** emerged in the United States in the early 1900s to combat a growing concern over the influence of big business in politics.

# caucus



**What it is:** a specific method of election that takes place during the primary election cycle

**How it works:** During the primary election cycle, some states opt to use the caucus system. When a state chooses to caucus, it holds party meetings at various locations throughout the state. Once there, party members share their preference for the candidate running for office, either by ballot or by voice. In presidential elections, the party members select a candidate's delegates to send to the national convention. These delegates then cast their votes for their pledged candidate at the convention to determine the party's nominee for president. There are only a small number of states that use this method of election.

**How it is used:** Traditionally, the Iowa **caucus** is the kickoff to the primary election cycle for president.

# Civil Rights Act of 1964



**What it is:** an act that created laws against the segregation and discrimination of minorities in the United States

**How it works:** A monumental piece of legislation, the Civil Rights Act of 1964 was pivotal in helping to establish equal rights for minorities in the United States. This act, signed into law by President Lyndon B. Johnson, brought an end to legal segregation in public places in the US. It also sought to end workplace discrimination by creating the U.S. Equal Employment Opportunity Commission. Additionally, it ended discrimination in federally funded projects and programs.

**How it is used:** The **Civil Rights Act of 1964** was originally proposed by President John F. Kennedy but was passed by President Johnson after Kennedy's death.

# closed primary



**What it is:** a type of primary election where only registered party members can vote

**How it works:** In the US election system, there are different types of primary elections. In a closed primary, only individuals who are registered with the political party can vote in that party's primary—for example, Democrats can vote only for Democratic candidates in the primary, and Republicans for Republican candidates. This ensures that only the people who are part of that political party are the ones voting for that party's candidates, eliminating crossover voting. It's up to the state government to determine whether to use a closed or an open primary.

**How it is used:** Currently, there are twelve states that use the **closed primary** system.

# conservative



**What it is:** a political ideology that falls to the right on the political spectrum

**How it works:** Conservative beliefs are rooted in individual liberty, limited federal government power, and traditionalism. They believe that a large government causes more problems than it helps. Individuals should retain the right to make choices in their businesses and private decisions without government interference. But the government should interfere in issues of morality, such as abortion. Conservatives believe that individuals should lift themselves up and not rely on government assistance, except in extreme cases. Accordingly, they believe government programs should be limited and taxes should be reduced. They also believe that a strong military is the best way to keep peace.

**How it is used:** The Republican Party in the United States maintains a **conservative** ideology.

# critical elections



**What it is:** an election where a political party experiences major changes in voter affiliations

**How it works:** During times of great social upheaval, critical elections can occur. These elections mark a significant shift in voter demographics. In turn, this can lead to important changes in a party's policy agenda and voting patterns in the future. For example, the election of 1932 took place during the Great Depression. Many people voted for President Franklin D. Roosevelt, the Democratic candidate, and his New Deal policies. With his victory, there was a shift in the makeup of the Democratic Party and the policies they would create for decades to come.

**How it is used:** Another **critical election** took place in 1980, when President Ronald Reagan came to power, marking a shift in the Republican Party toward a more conservative ideology.

# dark money



**What it is:** campaign spending by undisclosed donors meant to influence voters

**How it works:** In 2010, the Supreme Court ruled that corporations have political speech and can donate to campaigns. This led to the creation of super PACs, to which donors can give unlimited amounts of money. People then started creating shell companies, which funnel money into super PACs to be spent on campaigns. Dark money comes from these undisclosed donors and works to influence elections. Although people can see the name of a company that donated the money, they don't know who actually donated. This protects donors' identities, but it also keeps voters from knowing who's actually funding political messages.

**How it is used:** Other groups that are considered **dark money** groups include politically active nonprofits, such as social welfare organizations, which don't have to disclose their donors or spending.

# Democratic Party



**What it is:** the US political party that supports a more liberal political ideology

**How it works:** The Democratic Party was founded in 1828 and is the oldest continuously operating party in the United States. It adheres to the liberal political ideology. Democrats support more progressive government policies, advocating for civil rights for minorities, social welfare programs for families, and environmental protections programs. Today, Democrats are pro-choice, pro-same-sex marriage, and pro–gun regulation. Some groups that tend to be Democrats include women, Black voters, college graduates, and younger voters. But not all people in these demographic groups are Democrats.

**How it is used:** A **Democrat** in Congress pushed for legislation that supported efforts to stop the effects of pollution.

# disenfranchisement



**What it is:** the process of implementing policies that make it difficult for a group of people to vote

**How it works:** Disenfranchisement essentially means taking away someone's right to vote. The most prevalent example of this is when the Southern states passed voting laws with the intention to make it nearly impossible for African Americans to vote. To vote, you had to pass a literacy test, proving you could read and write, and pay a poll tax (a fee to vote), among other requirements. They also enforced grandfather clauses that stated if you or your ancestors could vote before the end of the Civil War, then you didn't have to complete the other requirements. These all ended in the 1960s.

**How it is used:** Some argue that **disenfranchisement** still happens with different voter qualifications, such as voter ID laws.

# electioneering



**What it is:** the active effort of different groups to promote a certain candidate, party, or issue during an election

**How it works:** During an election, many groups work to convince voters to vote for a certain candidate or ballot issue. These groups are practicing electioneering. Strategies used to convince voters include displaying campaign signs, creating TV or radio ads, sending out pamphlets and information about a candidate, and going door-to-door. Other examples of electioneering are hosting rallies or attending major community events to inform voters about a political party or candidate. Any action taken to earn the vote of someone is considered electioneering.

**How it is used:** Most states have laws that prohibit groups from **electioneering** too close to a polling location on Election Day.


# Electoral College



**What it is:** the process through which Americans elect their president

**How it works:** Every four years, Americans indirectly elect a president, either someone new or someone seeking a second term. Each state is assigned a number of electors, the people who officially cast the vote for president. This number is decided by the number of representatives and senators that each state has in Congress (with the exception of Washington, DC). When Americans vote on Election Day, they're actually selecting the electors who are pledged to their preferred candidate. In December, the electors chosen by the voters meet to cast the official votes for president. In January, the president of the Senate formally counts the electoral votes in Washington, DC. The candidate that receives a majority of electoral votes—at least 270—wins the presidency.

**How it is used:** Although the **Electoral College** doesn't meet until one month after the general election, Americans know who the next president will be before because of the country's winner-take-all system and the lack of faithless electors (defined in this chapter).

# endorsement



**What it is:** a public declaration of support for a certain candidate

**How it works:** In the American political system, name recognition plays an important role in elections. Because of this, individuals seek political endorsements from well-known politicians, as well as other popular figures in society, as a way to gain voter support. The strategy of endorsements is a way for a campaign to get people out to vote, improve credibility with voters, and attract media attention. Over time, campaigns have placed a larger emphasis on celebrity endorsements for candidates.

**How it is used:** Many Americans who don't have time to research candidates and their platforms use **endorsements** as a shortcut to understand the candidate.

# exit polls



**What it is:** public opinion polls that take place as one exits the polling location

**How it works:** On Election Day, news organizations are anxious for any information they can gather about the outcome of the election. Many of these groups conduct exit polls at polling stations to try and assess the possible outcome of the election. As ballots are anonymous, the exit polls can give some insight into how people are voting and help the media predict winners. Exit polls also give an understanding of how certain groups are voting on Election Day.

**How it is used:** As many states have pivoted to absentee ballots, methods for **exit polls** have shifted to include text, email, and phone surveys.

# faithless electors



**What it is:** people in the Electoral College who don't vote for their party's candidate

**How it works:** Prior to Election Day, each political party in each state selects the potential electors of the Electoral College, usually chosen for their commitment and loyalty to their political party. These individuals pledge to vote for their party's candidate for president and vice president. Occasionally, electors don't do what is expected of them and vote for a different candidate. This is known as being a faithless elector and casting a deviant vote, which has happened ninety times for the president and seventy-five times for the vice president. Most of the time, it was because a party's nominee died.

**How it is used:** To date, **faithless electors** have not affected the outcome of a presidential election.

# Federal Election Commission



**What it is:** the federal agency that monitors campaign spending to ensure accountability and fair elections across the country

**How it works:** In an effort to keep elections as fair as possible, the Federal Election Commission's job is to enforce campaign finance laws. It does this in a variety of ways, including requiring political campaigns to disclose donors and expenses, investigating complaints, and conducting audits of campaigns. The Federal Election Commission is bipartisan, meaning that it's made up of people from both political parties to keep it balanced. This group helps to create transparency in American elections.

**How it is used:** The only elections the **Federal Election Commission** oversees are the elections of president, vice president, and the United States Congress.

# front-loading



**What it is:** the process of moving up primary elections to increase a state's influence on the selection of a presidential candidate

**How it works:** The primary election cycle for the president in the United States takes place before the national conventions for each party. Generally, primary elections are held 6–9 months prior to the general election. Earlier primaries receive media attention, which can then affect how voters in other states choose to cast their votes. The process of front-loading is when states move their elections earlier in the year to have a larger impact on the selection of a presidential candidate. As a result, most states hold their primaries within the first four months of the year.

**How it is used:** Due to **front-loading**, the campaign season is shorter for candidates, making it harder for lesser-known candidates to raise sufficient funds and gain popularity by the primary election.

# gender gap



**What it is:** the long-standing difference in political views and perspectives between women and men

**How it works:** In every presidential election since 1980, there has been a distinct gap between how men and women vote. This is known as the gender gap. This can be traced to differing attitudes and priorities when it comes to politics. The gender gap fluctuates each election, depending on the candidates. Since 1996, women have overwhelmingly preferred Democrat candidates. But a majority of white women, though slight in some elections, have voted for the Republican candidate since the 2000 election.

**How it is used:** In the 2024 presidential election, the **gender gap** was 10 percentage points, with 45 percent of women and 55 percent of men voting for President Donald Trump.

# general election



**What it is:** voting selection that determines the winner for government positions

**How it works:** In the US political system, there are different types of elections. The general election refers to the election where voters select the winner for different government positions. Typically, this election refers to the presidential election, but it can also be used in reference to elections for all government positions. This term is used in local, state, and federal elections. There's a national general election every two years for members of Congress (every seat in the House and one-third of the Senate) and one every four years for the president. Local and state elections vary in their frequency.

**How it is used:** The **general election** for federal government positions takes place on the first Tuesday after the first Monday of November.

# grandfather clause



**What it is:** a policy passed in many states that allowed only people who could vote before a certain date to participate in elections

**How it works:** After the Reconstruction era ended, many Southern states worked to disenfranchise African-American voters. Although the 15th Amendment protected male voters of all races, state governments could pass voter qualifications that made it more challenging for certain groups to vote. The grandfather clause was one of these laws. Under this clause, if people or their ancestors could vote prior to a certain date, they were grandfathered into the new laws, meaning they didn't have to comply with the requirements. This essentially forced all African-American men who were enslaved and couldn't vote prior to 1870 to meet the other qualifications to vote.

**How it is used:** The **grandfather clause** was ruled as unconstitutional in 1915 and was abolished with the Voting Rights Act of 1965.

# grassroots lobbying



**What it is:** a political strategy of organizing the public in an effort to influence public officials

**How it works:** Grassroots lobbying is when a group works to organize a large number of people to contact their representatives to influence how they vote on certain issues. This strategy seeks to put pressure on government officials through social media, rallies, protests, public meetings, and petitions. Not only do grassroots lobbyists work to directly influence government officials, but they also attempt to affect public opinion on an issue, in the hopes of influencing the legislators who make policy.

**How it is used:** Many special interest groups like the American Association of Retired Persons (AARP) and the National Rifle Association (NRA) use the strategy of **grassroots lobbying** to attempt to influence public policy.

# hard money



**What it is:** political spending that is disclosed and limited

**How it works:** In campaign finance, there are different types of money. Hard money refers to more traditional campaign and political spending. With hard money, there's a lot of transparency. Donors must be disclosed and contribution limits are enforced. Organizations that spend hard money can work with the candidate to create materials that influence voters. These organizations include a candidate's committee, political parties, and political action committees. If you ever donate to a candidate specifically, you're giving them hard money that they can spend directly on their campaign.

**How it is used: Hard money** spending is largely outweighed by outside spending, like dark money, in American elections.

# horse race journalism



**What it is:** the emphasis of a candidate's popularity by the media

**How it works:** During the election cycle, there are many public opinion polls that seek to give insight into how Americans feel about a variety of issues and candidates. Media specialists use these polls to report on a candidate's popularity. But these polls, and public opinion, can change rapidly. So, when the media reports on the popularity of candidates, they often sound like an announcer of a horse race, with one candidate in the lead one day and another the next. This practice focuses on public perception of the candidate as opposed to the candidate's qualifications and stance on major issues.

**How it is used:** A result of **horse race journalism** is to make the election seem like a competitive game by emphasizing the public's changing opinion on candidates.

# incumbent



**What it is:** a person running for reelection

**How it works:** Anytime someone is running for reelection, they're known as an incumbent. In the federal government, only the elected position of president has term limits. Members of Congress can run for office as many times as they like. When incumbents run for office, they have a distinct advantage over other candidates. First, they have the power of name recognition, meaning the public is already familiar with them. These candidates have also already been doing the job and can reference their accomplishments in office. These factors help incumbents raise money for their campaigns, giving them an advantage over their opponents.

**How it is used:** Elections in Congress favor **incumbents**, with 96.6 percent of incumbents in the House of Representatives and 88 percent in the Senate winning reelections in 2024.

# independent



**What it is:** a person who doesn't adhere to a political party

**How it works:** Independents are a growing group in the United States, as more people disassociate with the Republican and Democratic Parties. Independents vote based on issues and don't tie themselves to a specific candidate or party. Most independents identify as moderate, meaning they might align with ideologies from both major political parties. Independents tend to cross party lines to vote, voting for Democrats, Republicans, and third parties depending on the candidate's stance on issues.

**How it is used:** In 2024, 42 percent of registered voters in the United States identified themselves as **independents**.

# initiative



**What it is:** the process of citizens placing proposed laws onto the ballot

**How it works:** Many states in the US have the initiative process, which allows citizens to place possible legislation onto the ballot to be voted on. This process requires citizens to obtain a certain number of signatures from registered voters and then file the proposed law with state officials. Direct initiatives are placed directly on the ballot for citizens to vote on. If a direct initiative passes, it becomes law. Indirect initiatives go to the legislature first. If the legislature doesn't pass the initiative, it's then placed on the ballot for a vote. This process allows citizens to create laws they want to see in action.

**How it is used:** There are over twenty states that have the **initiative** process, including some that allow citizens to propose constitutional amendments in addition to possible laws.

# interest groups



**What it is:** groups that work to influence public policy but don't seek office themselves

**How it works:** In the United States, interest groups are a way to link the American public with the government. Interest groups are focused on a specific issue, group of people, or ideology. These groups support candidates for office but don't run for office. Interest groups try to influence people already in office and to get people who support their mission into office. They use different strategies to do this, including direct lobbying, grassroots lobbying, litigation, campaign donations, and electioneering. Interest groups are incredibly powerful in politics, as they're policy specialists who can explain specific issues better than political parties can.

**How it is used:** Many Americans are members of **interest groups**, with two of the largest being the AARP and the NRA.

# liberal



**What it is:** a political ideology that falls to the left on the political spectrum

**How it works:** Liberal beliefs are rooted in equality under the law for all groups. Liberals believe that a larger government is necessary to combat the problems of the country. They support establishing more government assistance programs to help those in need; raising taxes, particularly on the wealthy; and increasing government intervention in businesses to discourage discrimination and to promote equality in the workplace and for consumers. Liberals don't support government interference, however, in personal moral decisions, as morals can be derived from religion and everyone can have different beliefs.

**How it is used:** The Democratic Party in the United States maintains a **liberal** political ideology.

# Libertarian Party



**What it is:** a third party in the United States focused on freedom

**How it works:** The Libertarian Party is the largest third party, or minor party, in the United States. Libertarians promote the idea that individuals should be free to live as they wish, so long as they don't interfere with the same rights as others. The government should be extremely limited in its ability to act on the people and businesses. Libertarians promote a free market economy with limited intervention from the government, including less taxation and regulations. They believe individuals have the right to privacy, both from the government and in their personal choices.

**How it is used:** One of the most famous members of the **Libertarian Party** was Ron Paul, who ran for president in 1988 with the party's endorsement.

# linkage institutions



**What it is:** the groups that connect the people with the policymaking process

**How it works:** In the United States, it can be challenging for citizens to have a direct connection to the government. But many people have access to the government through linkage institutions like political parties, interest groups, and the media. These groups serve to connect people to the government by providing information on major issues, news, and events that people might otherwise not have known about. Linkage institutions play an important role in the democratic system by giving the people a link to the government.

**How it is used:** People should connect with multiple **linkage institutions** to ensure they have a well-rounded picture of the government.

# lobbyist



**What it is:** a person actively influencing policy through direct contact with government officials

**How it works:** The act of lobbying is common in the US government. Lobbyists come from interest groups, major corporations, state and local governments, and other organizations to influence members of Congress, as well as the president, to vote a specific way on certain issues. These groups attempt to influence the policymaking process through their expertise on issues and their connections with other groups in government. Lobbyists must register with the government and can't use bribes or favors to influence members of the government.

**How it is used:** There are over ten thousand registered **lobbyists** operating in Washington, DC.

# midterm election



**What it is:** the election that takes place in the middle of a president's term

**How it works:** The president is elected every four years, but some members of Congress are up for reelection every two years, including all members of the House of Representatives and one-third of the Senate. These elections are known as midterm elections. Voter turnout is lower in midterm elections than in presidential elections, but midterms can be an indicator of how Americans feel about the president. Sometimes, there's a shift in party representation in Congress that can be traced back to voters' frustration with the president and their policies.

**How it is used:** Political scientists dictate that the president's party will lose votes in the **midterm election**.

# national convention



**What it is:** the meeting of political party members to formally nominate their candidate for president

**How it works:** Every presidential election cycle, each party holds a national convention to select the presidential candidate. In order to determine how many delegates each candidate will have at the convention, primary elections take place from January to June of the election year. At the convention, those delegates cast their votes to formally select the party's nominee for president. During these events, the party establishes its platform for the upcoming election, and popular party members give speeches about the issues and the presidential nominee to drum up support. Although the two major parties have different conventions, their goals are similar: nominate a candidate for president, establish goals for the election, and support their initiatives.

**How it is used:** Thousands of people attend the **national conventions**, which last for multiple days and are televised.

# National Voter Registration Act



**What it is:** an act of Congress that helped more Americans register to vote

**How it works:** In most states, people have to register to vote. In 1993, Congress passed the National Voter Registration Act in an effort to increase voter turnout by making it easier for citizens to register to vote. Under this act, nicknamed the Motor Voter Act, all states must provide citizens with the ability to register to vote when they're renewing or receiving their driver's license. Additionally, this law allows for mail-in applications for registration. Some states are exempt from this law, as they don't require registration to vote or they allow for registration on Election Day.

**How it is used:** After the **National Voter Registration Act** was passed, there was a large increase in voter registrations across the country.

# open primary

*anyone can vote*

**What it is:** a type of primary election where anyone can vote

**How it works:** In the US election system, there are different types of primary elections. In an open primary, anyone who is registered can vote. People don't have to be registered party members to receive a ballot. In most states, voters choose the ballot of whichever party they want to select candidates for. This allows voters who don't align with a political party, such as independents, to still have a voice in the primary elections.

**How it is used:** When Olivia, an independent, goes to vote in the **open primary**, she simply tells the poll worker which party's ballot she would like to cast her vote for, without having to show proof that she is a registered party member.

# party identification

*which party people identify with*

**What it is:** the process of people aligning themselves to a political party

**How it works:** Party identification, also known as party affiliation, is mostly between the Democratic and Republican Parties in the United States. Although there are third parties, most people identify themselves as a member of one of the two major parties, while some people prefer to say that they lean toward a particular party. Party identification can be seen as a form of social identity, especially as politics take up a large portion of the media.

**How it is used: Party identification** allows candidates to understand voter trends and to strategize during campaigns.

# political action committees



**What it is:** certain groups that raise and spend money specifically for campaigns

**How it works:** Political action committees, or PACs, focus on advancing the policy initiatives of the groups they represent by supporting candidates who will likely pass legislation they favor. They do this by raising money and spending it on campaign materials that support specific candidates. Most PACs are affiliated with a specific group, such as an interest group, corporation, labor union, or candidate's campaign. PACs are monitored by the federal government and must disclose all donors and expenses. There are also limits on how much people can donate to them.

**How it is used:** There are many types of **political action committees**, all with different rules related to their organization, structure, and fundraising.


# political efficacy



**What it is:** a person's belief that they can influence the political process

**How it works:** Political efficacy refers to a person's belief that they can make a change in the government. With high political efficacy, people feel like their vote counts, that their voice is being heard, and that they can invoke change in the political world. In this instance, people feel like they truly understand the political processes of their government and their role in that process. They also might feel like they understand how to effectively research candidates and complex political issues.

**How it is used:** Research shows that many Americans, particularly young people, are experiencing low **political efficacy**.

# political ideology

*a set of political beliefs*

**What it is:** a coherent set of values and beliefs about politics and government

**How it works:** There are many political ideologies, different from political parties, that can be found on the political spectrum. In fact, there can be multiple political parties that have the same or similar ideologies. The most common political ideologies in the US are liberal and conservative, although moderate ideology is growing among citizens. People with strong political ideologies are the most likely to participate in their government.

**How it is used:** The two major political parties in the United States use the liberal and conservative **political ideologies** to form policy.

# political party

*putting ideology in action*

**What it is:** a group that attempts to create policy that supports a certain political ideology

**How it works:** Political parties are the groups that make politics happen. The main functions of political parties are to recruit, nominate, and elect people who share their ideology into government positions. Political parties organize diverse groups of people into supporting one candidate for office. They also help political campaigns by raising money, hosting campaign events, and giving information to the community about candidates. Once candidates are in office, political parties work to pressure government officials to pass policies that support their ideology. Congress itself is organized on the basis of political party.

**How it is used:** In the United States, the **political party** with the minority in the White House or in Congress serves as a watchdog, making sure the other doesn't abuse its power.

# political polarization



**What it is:** political party ideology shifting to more extreme views

**How it works:** When political polarization occurs, ideologies move further away from the center of the political spectrum. Polarization is complicated and the reasons behind its occurrence are difficult to pinpoint. It can be attributed to policies of the election, biases within a group, demonization of the opposition, and the echo chambers of social media. When polarization happens, it's harder for government officials to reach compromises and policy gridlock becomes more common. Polarization can make citizens distrust the government and people of the opposite party as well.

**How it is used:** The United States is experiencing **political polarization** at an increasing rate compared to past decades.

# political socialization



**What it is:** the process of developing a political identity

**How it works:** Political socialization happens to every person, whether they're interested in politics or not. This process happens when ideas about politics and government are passed on to others. The most influential agent of political socialization is family. Children often possess the same values and ideologies as their parents, especially if their parents are aligned. Other agents of socialization include peers, school, and the media. This doesn't mean that individuals adopt all the same ideas as those around them. Rather, individuals learn about things from these groups and then develop their own ideas based on those influences.

**How it is used:** Social media is rising as an influential tool in young people's **political socialization**.

# poll tax



**What it is:** a fee individuals were forced to pay in order to vote

**How it works:** After the Reconstruction era ended, many Southern states worked to disenfranchise African-American voters. One way they did this was by instituting a poll tax, which required people to pay a tax in order to vote. This tax greatly affected poorer citizens, many African Americans included, and as a result, they couldn't vote. In the 1960s, the passage of the 24th Amendment ended poll taxes in federal elections, and the Voting Rights Act ended poll taxes in local and state elections.

**How it is used:** Due to grandfather clauses, African-American men were disproportionately affected by the **poll tax**, as many financially poor white men were exempt from paying it.

# polling location



**What it is:** the place people go to vote on Election Day

**How it works:** Oftentimes referred to as the polls, polling locations are where individuals go to cast their ballot on Election Day, or earlier in the several states that allow early voting. Per the 10th Amendment, states conduct elections and therefore can determine the rule and regulations for polling locations. Every state has different rules, but most states don't allow electioneering within a certain distance of the polling location. This can include, in some states, wearing apparel that supports a party or a candidate when you go to vote. As each state and locality have different rules, it's important to know where your polling location is before you go to vote.

**How it is used:** During the 2016 election, there were nearly 117,000 **polling locations** across the United States.

# precinct



**What it is:** a smaller area within a larger political district

**How it works:** During an election, larger political areas—counties, cities, or districts—are broken down into smaller precincts. People then vote within their precinct. Breaking down larger areas into smaller precincts can offer more accountability in elections. Smaller voting groups help to eliminate voter fraud, while also allowing for more efficiency related to the administration of elections and the collection of data from elections. These smaller groups leave less room for errors during the election process. This data can be used to target areas of low voter turnout and strategize for future elections. Precinct data can also be used to ensure that elections are fair.

**How it is used:** There are over 170,000 **precincts** in the United States.

# primary election



**What it is:** the election that determines who the official candidates for the party will be

**How it works:** Before the general election takes place, political parties hold primary elections. These elections allow voters to select their favorite candidate for that position from a pool of options, giving voters more of a voice. The winner of the primary election then becomes that party's candidate in the general election. Primary elections are held for the president, Congress, and state and local positions. There are different types of primary elections including closed, open, and top-two elections.

**How it is used:** Although **primary elections** are important, voter turnout for these elections is much lower than for the general election.

# prospective voting



**What it is:** casting your vote based on a candidate's platform and vision

**How it works:** During a campaign, many candidates make promises of what they plan to do when they're in office. When individuals vote for a candidate based on these promises, it's called prospective voting. People are basing their decision on their expectations of the candidate and how they'll perform in the role they're being elected to. Typically, when people vote for someone other than an incumbent, they're practicing prospective voting.

**How it is used: Prospective voting** is often more widely used in elections where major hot-button issues are at the forefront of the campaign.

# public opinion polls



**What it is:** surveys conducted to understand public opinion on a wide range of issues

**How it works:** Public opinion polls are used in a variety of ways and purposes. These surveys give insight into how Americans are feeling about major issues, and they also serve as a tool for candidates in their campaigns. Politicians can use these polls to influence their decision-making and their tactics for reelection. Not all public opinion polls are valid though. Effective polling uses a random, but representative, sample or group of people, with only a small margin of error. Additionally, the questions need to be valid and not leading in nature.

**How it is used: Public opinion polls** conducted by news organizations tend to be unreliable as they consider only the opinions of the viewers of that station.

# ranked choice voting



**What it is:** a system of voting where individuals rank their preferred candidates

**How it works:** With ranked choice voting, individuals select their top candidates for an elected position and rank their first, second, and third choices. If their first choice doesn't win, their vote then goes to their second choice. This process allows voters to have more of a voice in the voting process. Even if their first choice doesn't win, they still have a say in the election. Ranked choice also gives third-party candidates more of a chance to gain votes. Overall, this system of voting opens up the voting process to be more representative of the people's wants.

**How it is used:** There are a number of states, including Alaska and Maine, that use **ranked choice voting** for local and state elections in the United States.

# rational choice voting



**What it is:** a theory that suggests voters make decisions based on who will serve their own self-interest

**How it works:** When voters go to the polls on Election Day, they are there to decide who will lead their government. With rational choice voting, individuals have investigated the issues and the impacts on their daily lives. They've looked into the candidates and their stances. Rational choice voters look for the candidate who will best serve their own self-interests and who will benefit them the most. Rational choice voters aren't necessarily looking at the big picture or the common good but rather whose policies will be most favorable for the individual voter.

**How it is used: Rational choice voting** can impact how candidates structure their campaigns, as they'll cater to the interests of these individuals in order to gain votes.

# recall election



**What it is:** an election where citizens can vote to remove an elected official from office before their term has been served

**How it works:** In some states, if citizens are upset or frustrated with an elected official at the local or state level, they can attempt to remove them from office by instigating a recall election. To do this, they must file a petition with a certain number of signatures. Should they receive enough signatures, an election is held where voters decide if the official should remain in office. This process gives the people a check on the state and local governments' power—federal officials can't be recalled.

**How it is used:** In some **recall elections**, voters can also vote for the official's replacement in case the recall succeeds.

# referendum



**What it is:** when citizens vote on approval or rejection of laws proposed by state legislatures

**How it works:** The referendum allows citizens to vote to approve or reject laws that have been proposed by their state legislatures. Most of the time, this process is used to veto laws made by the legislature, called the veto referendum. To make this happen, signatures must be collected and verified. Then, the new law appears on the ballot for a vote. The law can't take effect until after citizens have approved it. If voters reject (veto) it, then the law doesn't take effect.

**How it is used:** There are over twenty states that have the **referendum** process.

# Republican Party



**What it is:** the US political party that supports a more conservative political ideology

**How it works:** The Republican Party, also known as the Grand Old Party, was founded in 1854 and adheres to the conservative ideology. Republicans support more traditional government policies. They support fewer regulations on businesses to promote economic growth, as well as cutting government spending and programs. Alongside a cut to government programs, Republicans support cutting taxes to help bolster the economy. They tend to adhere to traditional Christian values and don't support abortions or same-sex marriage. They are proponents of the 2nd Amendment and don't support intensive gun regulation.

**How it is used:** Groups who tend to be **Republican** include white men, older Americans, and religious individuals.

# retrospective voting



**What it is:** voting for a candidate because of what they did or didn't accomplish in office

**How it works:** When voters use retrospective voting, they look to a candidate's actions to see what that candidate has done in order to make their decisions. This type of voting is used especially when the candidate is an incumbent. If a voter is happy with the candidate's performance, they'll vote for them. If they're unhappy with their performance, they'll vote against them. Sometimes, voters also use retrospective voting by looking at political parties' actions to make decisions.

**How it is used: Retrospective voters** often look at actions relating to the economy, particularly when voting in presidential elections.

# revolving door politics



**What it is:** the movement of people between government and private industry jobs

**How it works:** The federal government works closely with a number of industries and interest groups in the United States. Sometimes, individuals who work for the government leave their positions and get a new job working for one of these groups, often one they worked closely with in their government role. At times, the revolving door leads from a government job to a lobbyist, where one can use their contacts to have an advantage over other lobbyists. Because of the possible ethical conflicts, Congress has issued mandatory cooling-off periods for government officials who become lobbyists.

**How it is used: Revolving door politics** also refers to individuals in the private industry moving into public (government) positions, where they might favor certain companies over others.

# single-issue group



**What it is:** a type of interest group that focuses on a singular issue

**How it works:** Single-issue groups are a type of interest group that focuses on one topic or concern in an effort to influence policy about that issue. These groups become policy experts and offer their expertise to members of Congress as they investigate the impact and possible outcomes of bills. Single-issue groups have the most success on nuanced, technical issues. These groups range in topics from gun rights to abortion to helping the unhoused. They use whatever tactics work best for the group but most often donate to campaigns or lobby members of Congress.

**How it is used:** EMILYs List, a **single-issue group** dedicated to getting pro-choice women elected to office, contributed over $4 million to the 2024 federal election.

# soft money



**What it is:** funds donated to political parties for a general purpose

**How it works:** Soft money was banned in the Bipartisan Campaign Reform Act of 2002. Before then, soft money referred to the undisclosed, unlimited amounts of money donated to political parties for broad purposes. This money was typically funneled out to party committees and used in various ways. There were no restrictions on its use, except that it couldn't be used to support federal candidates. But because the money was often used to bolster the party itself, it indirectly supported the candidate's platform.

**How it is used:** Although **soft money** donations are illegal, there are many other similar donations that are allowed.

# split-ticket voting



**What it is:** when a person votes for Democrats and Republicans on the same ballot

**How it works:** Split-ticket voting occurs when a person chooses different political parties for different positions on the same ballot. Voters who split their ballot tend to focus on the individual candidates and specific issues, voting based on their ideologies regardless of party. Most people who practice split-ticket voting identify themselves as independents and are moderate in their political ideology. This is the opposite of straight-ticket voting.

**How it is used:** **Split-ticket voting** was common in the twentieth century and led to outcomes where the presidential candidate a state chose was of a different party than the senator they elected.

# straight-ticket voting



**What it is:** when a person votes for only one political party on their ballot

**How it works:** If someone votes straight ticket, it means they've selected only members of a certain party for all offices during an election. In some states, voters can do this with one ballot selection. However, most states have tried to remove this option in their election systems, as it creates less informed voters who don't research the candidates or issues. Voters can still vote for one party, but they must individually select each candidate instead of the system selecting all members of the same party for them.

**How it is used: Straight-ticket voting** is a common practice among strong ideological voters who align with a certain political party.

# suffrage



**What it is:** the right to vote in political elections

**How it works:** Suffrage, also called enfranchisement, is a right that people have fought for over generations. In the beginning of this nation, only white property-owning men could vote. It took many years and many movements, but now, the majority of US citizens eighteen and older can vote in elections, with some exceptions. Most notably, in some states, convicted felons lose their right to vote.

**How it is used:** The 19th Amendment granted **suffrage** to women in 1920.

# superdelegate



**What it is:** a delegate of the Democratic National Convention who was not elected and has not pledged to support any specific candidate

**How it works:** In primary elections, voters cast ballots for their preferred political party candidate. The results of the primary determine how many delegates each candidate receives. These delegates are pledged to a specific candidate at the national convention. Superdelegates, though, aren't elected in the primary election. They're typically high-ranking members of the Democratic Party who attend the convention and can vote for whichever candidate they prefer. Over time, their impact has changed. In the past, superdelegates could influence the outcome of the primary election with their votes but not today. They can, however, influence the election by endorsing candidates.

**How it is used: Superdelegates** are typically Democratic members of Congress, governors, and former presidents.

# super PAC



**What it is:** a type of political action committee that people can donate unlimited amounts of money to

**How it works:** In 2010, the Supreme Court ruled on the case *Citizens United v. Federal Election Commission*. In this case, the court ruled that corporations have political speech and can't be limited in their donations to campaigns. This ruling opened the door for super PACs. Super PACs were created to advocate for the election of certain candidates through the use of funds donated by major corporations, businesses, individuals, and unions. Super PACs can raise unlimited funds and use that money to create materials for a candidate, but they can't coordinate with, or work directly with, the candidate.

**How it is used:** There are more than 2,500 **super PACs** registered with the Federal Election Commission.

# Super Tuesday



**What it is:** a day in the primary election cycle when many states hold their primaries or caucuses

**How it works:** Every state decides when it will hold its primary elections. Super Tuesday typically occurs in March, coinciding with the concept of front-loading, as states want the attention of having their primary early. Because so many convention votes can be won on this day, these elections tend to determine the front-runner for both parties. If a candidate doesn't win a good number of votes on Super Tuesday, they'll most likely drop out of the primary race, further solidifying the front-runner.

**How it is used:** The number of elections that take place on **Super Tuesday** fluctuates from year to year, with seventeen states holding Super Tuesday primaries in 2024.

# swing states



**What it is:** states where the outcome of the presidential election isn't clear

**How it works:** In the US, there are some states that have an overwhelming majority of Republican or Democratic voters. Because of this, presidential candidates spend more energy campaigning in the other states, where the outcome isn't easily predicted because there is no clear majority. These states become a major focus for candidates in an effort to swing them to one party over another. Due to the winner-take-all system of the Electoral College, swing states are highly competitive during presidential elections, as the margin between the two major parties is so close. Generally, these states also have more electoral votes.

**How it is used:** In the 2024 presidential election, **swing states** included Arizona, Georgia, Michigan, Nevada, Pennsylvania, and Wisconsin.

# think tank



**What it is:** a group that researches and develops public policy outside of the government

**How it works:** Think tanks are institutions that strive to promote certain public policies through research, analysis, and advocacy. They publish studies based on research about the need for certain policies, which can influence voters and members of Congress. They work with the government to develop policies by sharing their ideas with government officials for solutions to society's problems. Plus, they can act as a bridge between the worlds of academia and policymaking.

**How it is used:** Popular **think tanks** include the Brookings Institute and the Heritage Foundation.

# third party



**What it is:** a political party that is not one of the two major parties in the United States

**How it works:** Although third parties face an uphill battle when going against the two major parties in the US, they serve an important role in the political system. Third parties give Americans an alternative option if they don't support the Democratic or Republican Parties, keeping voters engaged and politically active. They can also draw attention to a policy area that major parties ignore. As third parties gain popularity for their ideas, there may be a shift in how the major parties operate, encouraging them to adopt the same philosophy and enact policies they otherwise wouldn't have.

**How it is used:** The most successful **third party** was Theodore Roosevelt's Progressive Party, also known as the Bull Moose Party.

# top-two primary



**What it is:** a type of primary election where all candidates, regardless of party, are on the same ballot

**How it works:** In the US election system, there are different types of primary elections. The top-two primary puts all candidates on the same ballot. This allows voters to choose the candidate they prefer in all positions, regardless of party, giving voters the option to cross party lines and vote for members of different parties in the primary election. These primaries also cater to people who don't affiliate with a certain party, as the system gives them more of an opportunity to vote that the closed or open primaries don't necessarily offer. In a top-two primary, the top-two candidates face each other in that state's general election.

**How it is used:** The **top-two primary** election is used by some states, like California and Washington, in their congressional and statewide elections.

# two-party system



**What it is:** the structure of a government system where two major parties dominate the political landscape

**How it works:** The United States is a two-party system. The Republican Party and Democratic Party are the country's two major parties. Third parties exist but find it hard to influence politics in a widespread way. Although two-party systems encourage stability through the consistency of the two parties, critics argue that it limits voter's choices and pushes alternative voices to the side. One component that helps maintain the two-party system in the US is winner-take-all elections that exist at all levels of government.

**How it is used:** The **two-party system** can create more moderate policies, as the two parties have to appeal to a wide range of voters.

# voter apathy



**What it is:** the lack of interest among voters in participating in politics

**How it works:** When people choose not to vote, they're experiencing voter apathy. This concept centers around the idea that people disengage from the political process and choose not to participate because of various factors. Everyone has their reasons, but people experiencing voter apathy tend to have low political efficacy (defined in this chapter). Many distrust the government and feel that they lack control in the political process, believing that government officials don't focus on constituents but turn instead toward interest groups. Others feel voter fatigue due to the high frequency of elections and political news.

**How it is used:** One group that experiences **voter apathy** is young adults, who also have the lowest voter turnout.

# voter registration



**What it is:** the process that someone takes to enroll to vote

**How it works:** Per the 10th Amendment, the states conduct elections. This includes the power to determine voter registration requirements. Each state has different processes for determining eligible voters. Most states require that you register to vote and some have specific deadlines for completing the process. Some states allow you to register on the day of the election; others have continuous registration, where you update your registration only if you move. Before Election Day, be sure to check out your state's voter registration rules.

**How it is used:** North Dakota is the only state that doesn't require **voter registration**.

# voter turnout



**What it is:** how much of the population actually votes in elections

**How it works:** Voter turnout rates provide important information about who's voting in elections and who isn't. Looking at voter turnout allows political campaigns to target different groups of people and think about how to encourage increased turnout. Recent shifts to more mail-in ballots and early voting have helped to increase voter turnout. But some qualified voters still don't vote, for reasons such as they don't care about politics, don't like the candidates, or are too busy.

**How it is used:** The 2024 presidential election had a **voter turnout** of 64 percent of the voting-eligible population, which was the second-highest turnout in the past century.

# Voting Rights Act



**What it is:** an act that eliminated voter discrimination laws and promoted equality in voting

**How it works:** In 1965, President Lyndon B. Johnson signed the Voting Rights Act into law. This law served to eliminate voter discrimination laws that predominantly targeted African Americans. It makes literacy tests, grandfather clauses, and poll taxes in state elections illegal. It also provides provisions to make voting more easily accessible to minority groups—for example, printing ballots in multiple languages, assisting people with disabilities when they vote, and sending federal examiners to areas with low voter registration rates for minority voters.

**How it is used:** The **Voting Rights Act** was passed after years of peaceful protests enacted by the Civil Rights Movement, including such events as Freedom Summer and the Selma to Montgomery march.

# winner-take-all system



**What it is:** the political system in which the candidate who wins the most votes gets all the electoral votes or available seats

**How it works:** In the United States, the winner-take-all system is used in presidential elections and in elections for members of Congress. When a candidate for president wins the popular vote in a state, that candidate receives all the state's electoral votes, even if the vote was close. This is true for all states except Maine and Nebraska, which use a different, more proportional system. In the House elections, candidates who win a majority of the votes represent the entire district. This system makes it challenging for all voices to be represented.

**How it is used:** A major criticism of the **winner-take-all system** is that it doesn't always represent what the people want, and sometimes the majority vote of the country doesn't match the winner of the Electoral College.

# Chapter 7

# CIVIL LIBERTIES AND THE MEDIA

The United States is the land of the free but without context, this might feel like a vague sentiment. This chapter explores the fundamental rights and freedoms that all US citizens have thanks to the Bill of Rights in the Constitution. Although these rights are seemingly simple, the complexity of these freedoms have been interpreted through court cases and law over centuries. This chapter seeks to explain the freedoms and protections granted to all citizens while also explaining their limitations.

One of the protections outlined in the Bill of Rights is the freedom of the press. The press is often called the fourth branch of government due to its pivotal role in informing citizens and reporting on government actions. As the US has grown and technology has advanced, so has the media. This complicated, far-reaching entity affects all citizens and their interpretation of the government. This chapter aims to explain the liberties all Americans have and also define many of the terms associated with the media and the role it plays in American government.

# affirmative action



**What it is:** a policy designed to target the consequences of previous discrimination by giving special consideration to individuals

**How it works:** Affirmative action began in the 1960s when President John F. Kennedy passed an executive order establishing that government contractors must take affirmative action to eliminate discrimination in their hiring practices. From there, other institutions adopted similar practices, with some intentionally hiring people based on their race or gender in an effort to make up for past discriminatory practices. Affirmative action policies also strive to create a workforce that represents the diversity of the United States. Critics claim that affirmative action is reverse discrimination and keeps qualified people from getting jobs and being accepted to universities.

**How it is used:** With **affirmative action**, people must be qualified, as race or gender can't be the only factor for college admissions or for someone earning a job or promotion.

# assembly



**What it is:** a freedom granted to Americans to gather in large groups

**How it works:** In the 1st Amendment to the Constitution, citizens are guaranteed the freedom of assembly. This means that people can gather in large groups for a variety of purposes. Most notably, it means that people can peacefully protest, have parades that serve as protests, and hold meetings to present ideas not supported by the government. Under the 1st Amendment, people can do these things without fear of punishment or retaliation by the government, but this freedom becomes unprotected when it escalates to violence.

**How it is used:** The 1937 Supreme Court case *DeJonge v. Oregon* ruled that people have the freedom of **assembly** at both the national and state levels of government.

# Bill of Rights



**What it is:** a list of fundamental rights and freedoms that individuals possess

**How it works:** During the debate over the ratification of the Constitution, the Anti-Federalists argued strongly that a Bill of Rights was needed. They believed that without this list, the government could trample on the rights of the people. In the end, the Anti-Federalists won this argument, and the first ten amendments to the Constitution were created. The Bill of Rights protects the people by limiting the power of the government; the government can't take these rights away without just cause.

**How it is used:** Originally, the **Bill of Rights** applied only to the national government, but over time it has been incorporated into the states.

# broadcast networks



**What it is:** the groups that send out media content to local stations that air it for free

**How it works:** Being the distributors of content, broadcast networks play an important role in the media. Their content reaches more people because it's aired for free and supported by advertising. People don't technically have to pay for broadcast network content if they can get enough signal for it with an antenna. As a result, this content attracts large audiences and can have a major effect on how people view the government and politics. But the rise of cable news networks has shifted the media landscape.

**How it is used:** Major **broadcast networks** include ABC, NBC, CBS, and Fox.

# civil liberties



**What it is:** the fundamental freedoms and rights that the government can't infringe upon

**How it works:** Although the civil liberties listed in the Bill of Rights are seemingly straightforward, challenges to these rights have still been introduced. The Supreme Court has heard a multitude of cases regarding people's civil liberties and has further defined what rights a person truly has and what the limitations on their civil liberties actually are. These interpretations also guide the government on what actions it can take related to Americans' civil liberties.

**How it is used: <u>Civil liberties</u>** help to protect one of the founding principles of the United States government—freedom.

# civil rights



**What it is:** protections from biases regarding race, sex, religion, national origin, and other characteristics

**How it works:** Civil rights work to protect the rights of minority groups and ensure equal protection under the law, a principle established in the 14th Amendment. Many groups have fought for civil rights throughout US history. One of the most famous movements is the Civil Rights Movement, when African Americans fought for equal rights and to end legal discrimination. Groups continue to fight for these rights today in an effort to establish a more equitable society.

**How it is used:** Civil liberties are protections from the government, but **<u>civil rights</u>** rely on the government to protect the people.

# compelled speech



**What it is:** speech that the government forces someone to make

**How it works:** Compelled speech is when the government forces an individual or group to issue a statement that the government has approved. Because citizens have the right to free speech under the 1st Amendment, compelled speech isn't permitted in the United States. The compelled speech doctrine protects citizens from being punished by the government for refusing to comply, support, or agree with a government-issued statement. For example, students in school can't be forced to stand for the Pledge of Allegiance, and they can't be punished for refusing to do so.

**How it is used:** In 1977, the Supreme Court ruled to uphold the **compelled speech** doctrine by ruling that the state of New Hampshire couldn't punish a man who covered up the state motto on his license plate.

# confirmation bias



**What it is:** a tendency to seek out information that reinforces one's own beliefs

**How it works:** It's human nature to find information that supports the beliefs you hold. Confirmation bias in politics, however, can lead to polarization and distrust of the opposition. This happens more frequently today due to social media and the increasing partisanship of media outlets. Individuals tend to get their news from media outlets that support their political leanings, thereby confirming their bias. This trend can also lead to people spreading fake news since people share stories that support their views, even ones that are untrue. Additionally, people begin to distrust the news more if it doesn't present information that they agree with.

**How it is used:** Ways to combat **confirmation bias** include seeking out various news sources, fact-checking news outlets, and talking to others to gain diverse perspectives.

# consumer-driven media



**What it is:** the tendency of news outlets to focus on the consumer over the content

**How it works:** The consumer plays an important role in the media landscape. News outlets are driven to focus on what consumers want, leading them to shape their media to attract more likes, clicks, and shares. This practice also gives consumers the power to drive the narrative of the news, as the media caters to their audience. Consumer-driven media shifts the emphasis away from the media being a one-way flow of information and to the consumers being in charge of the creation and distribution of information.

**How it is used: Consumer-driven media** can lead to questions of reliability and quality when it comes to information distributed on the Internet.

# cruel and unusual punishment



**What it is:** a punishment that is unfit for the crime committed

**How it works:** The 8th Amendment to the Constitution protects citizens from cruel and unusual punishment, meaning the punishment must fit the crime. Punishments for crimes in the United States can include fines, community service, and imprisonment. Severe crimes can also lead to the death penalty (capital punishment). Although critics of the death penalty argue that it's cruel and unusual, the Supreme Court has ruled that the death penalty can be a violation of the 8th Amendment only when sentencing someone with an intellectual disability, someone with a severe mental illness, or someone who was a minor when their crime was committed.

**How it is used:** It would be considered **cruel and unusual punishment** for someone to receive the death penalty for a minor offense.

# double jeopardy



**What it is:** being charged for the same, overt crime more than once

**How it works:** The 5th Amendment to the Constitution protects citizens from double jeopardy. This protection ensures that an individual isn't charged for the same crime twice. If a person has been put on trial and found innocent, they can't be tried again for that crime, even if there's new evidence. They can be tried, however, in a different type of court. Someone can be brought up on criminal charges for a specific action and then sued in civil court for the same act.

**How it is used:** If someone is acquitted of a robbery but then commits another robbery, indicting them on the same charges is not a violation of **double jeopardy**.

# due process



**What it is:** a policy that ensures all citizens experience the same process when dealing with the government

**How it works:** The 5th and 14th Amendments guarantee due process for all citizens. Procedural due process guarantees that the government follows certain procedures when taking away someone's rights. This form of due process is used in investigations, arrests, and trial proceedings. Substantive due process guarantees that all laws will be fair and will not unreasonably intrude on people's right to privacy. For example, people have rights such as the right to marry, to be a parent, and to work an ordinary job.

**How it is used:** Procedural **due process** includes such things as probable cause, search and arrest warrants, Miranda warnings, and the right to a trial by jury.

# eminent domain



**What it is:** the right of the government to seize a person's property for its own use

**How it works:** The 5th Amendment protects people's right to property, but it also allows the government to take someone's private property for public use. This exception is known as eminent domain. For example, if the government is building a public park or an interstate highway and needs land, it can take a person's property as long as it pays them fair compensation. Eminent domain was originally allowed only for public works, but the Supreme Court ruled in 2005 that governments can use eminent domain for private development projects if the goal of those projects is to stimulate the local economy.

**How it is used:** In 1896, the United States government implemented **eminent domain** and took the Gettysburg battlefield from the Gettysburg Electric Railway Company.

# Equal Protection Clause



**What it is:** a clause stopping states from denying any person equal protection of the law

**How it works:** Found in the 14th Amendment to the Constitution, the Equal Protection Clause guarantees equal treatment for all. This clause prohibits the states from discriminating against citizens without a valid reason. The Equal Protection Clause has been the basis for many civil rights cases, including *Brown v. Board of Education of Topeka*, which outlawed segregation in public schools. The Supreme Court has created different levels of scrutiny to determine where a law or action violates this clause. See *scrutiny tests* in this chapter for more information.

**How it is used:** If a person believes that a law violates the **Equal Protection Clause**, they can file a lawsuit against the government.

# Establishment Clause

*separation of church and state*

**What it is:** a clause in the 1st Amendment that prohibits the government from establishing a national religion

**How it works:** Part of the 1st Amendment to the Constitution is the concept of freedom of religion. The Establishment Clause promotes this freedom by preventing the federal or state governments from prioritizing one religion over another. Because the United States has no national religion, the Establishment Clause has been interpreted to require a separation between the church and the state. The government can't force individuals to attend religious events or punish people for not aligning themselves with a specific religion. Additionally, the government shouldn't actively involve itself in religious activity, nor can it be hostile to religion. When it comes to religion, the government should be neutral.

**How it is used:** Public schools can't teach religious doctrine, per the **Establishment Clause**, but they can teach about the customs, practices, and history of different religions in a secular way.

# exclusionary rule

*can't use illegally collected evidence*

**What it is:** a legal rule stating evidence collected illegally is inadmissible in court

**How it works:** The exclusionary rule was applied to all governments by the Supreme Court case *Mapp v. Ohio*. The ruling determined that evidence collected without a warrant or by illegal means can't be used in court, even if it's particularly incriminating. The 4th Amendment protects citizens from unreasonable searches and seizures. This rule helps to stop the government from abusing its power by prohibiting illegal searches, with some exceptions. Generally, if a warrant isn't used to collect evidence, the evidence can't be used in a trial.

**How it is used:** If a defendant feels the **exclusionary rule** was violated, they can file a motion to keep evidence from being used in trial.

# Free Exercise Clause

*freedom to practice religion*

**What it is:** clause in the 1st Amendment that grants citizens the right to practice whichever religion they choose

**How it works:** Part of the 1st Amendment is the concept of freedom of religion. The Free Exercise Clause dictates that all individuals have the freedom to practice any religion they choose, including no religion at all. People have the right to celebrate religious holidays and, in most cases, to take time off work to do so. There are limitations to this freedom: You can't break the law and claim it's in the name of your religion. For example, you cannot harm someone and claim you did so because your religion requires that action to take place. You also cannot practice bigamy, or have multiple spouses, in the name of your religion. Additionally, you can't deprive children of basic needs or education, citing religious reasons.

**How it is used:** The **Free Exercise Clause** allows individuals to wear religious attire, such as a cross or hijab, and also protects religious beliefs, like those of Jehovah's Witnesses refusing blood transfusions.

# free press

*open media*

**What it is:** the government can't regulate the press

**How it works:** The 1st Amendment guarantees that the press remains free from government control, meaning that news organizations can't be limited by the government. The government can't censor the news, nor can it punish news outlets for reporting on government activity. The media can criticize the government, satirize the government, and challenge the government. It can conduct investigations into government activity and report on its findings to the people. The only real limitations to this freedom are that the press can't put national security at risk or commit libel.

**How it is used:** A **free press** is an integral part of American democracy because without it the people wouldn't know what the government is doing.

# free speech

*freedom to say whatever you want*

**What it is:** people have the freedom to speak their minds

**How it works:** The 1st Amendment guarantees the freedom of speech for all citizens. This law allows people to speak their minds and openly criticize their government without fear of punishment. Speech encompasses more than just the spoken word; it also translates into expressions and beliefs. Different types of speech—such as political speech, symbolic speech, and commercial speech—are all protected. But there are some limitations to freedom of speech: Individuals can't incite a riot or violence, commit slander, make true threats, or use obscenities in a public forum.

**How it is used:** An example of **free speech** protected by the 1st Amendment is the burning of the American flag, which was determined to be a form of political speech and thereby protected in the Supreme Court case *Texas v. Johnson.*

# Freedom of Information Act

*transparency in the government*

**What it is:** an act that gives the public access to certain government records

**How it works:** Established in 1967, the Freedom of Information Act has worked to create openness and transparency between the government and its people. Using this act, individuals can request access to records from federal agencies. The agency is required to meet this request as long as the information doesn't fall into one of the nine exemptions, which include classified information for the protection of national security, issues of personal privacy, and law enforcement.

**How it is used:** Using the **Freedom of Information Act**, she was able to receive her great-grandfather's military service record.

# gatekeeping



**What it is:** the process of reporters filtering information being distributed by media outlets

**How it works:** News outlets determine the information that the people learn on a daily basis. One thing that happens with this responsibility is gatekeeping. With gatekeeping, the media determines what information the public needs to know. It filters out stories that it doesn't feel are as important and reports on the issues it thinks are most crucial for public consumption. This often leads to the media reporting on stories that it thinks its audience will prefer and stories that are of the public interest.

**How it is used: Gatekeeping** is typically done by the editors and publishers of major news outlets.

# habeas corpus



**What it is:** a writ that allows a person to question the legality of their detention before a judge

**How it works:** The writ of habeas corpus is an important protection for the people against the government. It ensures that the government can't arrest someone, put them in jail, and keep them there indefinitely. This law guarantees that individuals have a fair trial and due process. If a person files a writ of habeas corpus, the government must prove why their detainment is lawful.

**How it is used: Habeas corpus** can be suspended by Congress during times of invasion or rebellion.

# hate speech



**What it is:** a form of protected speech that demonstrates hatred toward a person or group of people based on their characteristics

**How it works:** The 1st Amendment guarantees freedom of speech, including hate speech. The courts have ruled that the government can't limit speech only for being offensive or hateful. There are, however, limitations to this. If hate speech is used to incite violence, it's not protected. Hate speech also can't be used in the form of harassment or true threats. The argument for allowing hate speech is a slippery slope. Once speech is limited in this way, it can lead to other limitations on speech that criticizes or dissents.

**How it is used: Hate speech**, while protected, can have a negative effect on society as it can make individuals feel targeted and fearful.

# imminent lawless action test



**What it is:** a test used to determine whether speech inciting illegal activity is protected or not

**How it works:** The imminent lawless action test was established through the 1969 Supreme Court case *Brandenburg v. Ohio*. This test helps determine when speech is no longer protected under the 1st Amendment. Speech that isn't protected by the test is speech that's intended to cause immediate illegal activity and is likely to do so. The speaker's intent is key for this test, as is the likelihood that the speech will result in lawless action. If someone's speech is found to violate this test, they can be prosecuted by the government.

**How it is used:** The **imminent lawless action test** replaced the clear and present danger test to better protect speech by placing a higher standard for what constitutes imminent incitement.

# investigative reporting



**What it is:** a type of journalism when reporters work to uncover government wrongdoings to expose them to the people

**How it works:** It's always the hope that the government is working in the people's best interest and not abusing its power, but sometimes that isn't the case. Investigative reporting works to expose the government's overreach of power to inform the public. In the United States, the people hold the power. As such, the people need to be informed of situations where their representatives aren't working for them. Investigative journalists research, conduct interviews, and write articles to inform people of what's happening so they can remain informed, active citizens.

**How it is used:** Two successful **investigative reporters** are Bob Woodward and Carl Bernstein, who worked to expose the government's role in the Watergate scandal.

# jawboning



**What it is:** the use of government power to pressure others to take actions that the government can't legally take

**How it works:** The 1st Amendment protects individuals from government censorship. Jawboning is the government's way to circumvent these protections to achieve a desired result, particularly when it comes to speech. Often, the government uses its regulatory power to convince companies to change their rules to better fit what the government wants. For example, many companies must be compliant with environmental regulations established by the government in order to limit pollution and its harmful effects on citizens. Jawboning is allowed if the government persuades a company to do something but not if it crosses the line into coercion. This can be determined by looking at the government's language, the company's interpretation of the language, and whether the government threatened the company with negative consequences if it didn't comply.

**How it is used:** Today, **jawboning** often occurs when government officials use social media to influence public behavior.

# libel

*writing hateful accounts about another*

**What it is:** writing untrue statements about someone with malicious intent

**How it works:** Although the 1st Amendment protects freedom of speech and freedom of the press, it doesn't protect libel. Libel occurs when someone knowingly writes falsehoods about another person with the intention of harming their reputation. The United States has strong libel laws, particularly for public officials; these laws protect journalists from accusations of libel in their reporting. To convict someone of committing libel, a person must prove that the author knew what they wrote was incorrect and that they had malicious intent to harm another person's reputation. Proving libel is incredibly difficult to do.

**How it is used:** **Libel** is a form of defamation that can occur in all print media, including magazines, newspapers, online posts, and blogs.

# narrowcasting

*tailored media content*

**What it is:** the media focuses on delivering content to one specific audience

**How it works:** Narrowcasting can be seen in the rise of twenty-four-hour cable news networks and their well-known political biases. These news networks are profit-driven entities that cater their stories to specific demographics rather than to a broad audience of various perspectives. With social media and the rise of the Internet, narrowcasting is becoming more prevalent. Content delivered through narrowcasting reinforces people's political opinions, contributes to a culture of confirmation bias, makes compromise more difficult, and increases polarization.

**How it is used:** Major news networks began **narrowcasting** in an attempt to make more money by catering to either a Republican or Democratic audience.

## obscene speech



**What it is:** a type of unprotected speech that's offensive in nature

**How it works:** Although the 1st Amendment protects many types of speech, obscene speech isn't protected. To determine whether speech is obscene, courts use the Miller test, established through the Supreme Court case *Miller v. California*. This test is used for all types of obscene speech—not just verbal speech. Speech is considered obscene if the average person perceives it as promoting excessive sexual interest compared to community standards, if the speech describes sexual activities in an offensive way as defined by law, and if the speech lacks serious literary, artistic, political, or scientific value.

**How it is used:** Child sexual abuse material violates all three parts of the Miller test, making it **obscene speech** and punishable by law.

## petition



**What it is:** the act of requesting the government to right a wrong

**How it works:** The 1st Amendment protects every citizen's right to petition the government. Petitioning the government comes in different forms, including contacting government officials to express opinions and concerns. Under this right, citizens have the power to sue the government if they believe a law or action has violated their constitutional rights. Citizens can file petitions with the government to initiate ballot measures or ask officials to take actions on issues. Protesting is also protected under the freedom of petition.

**How it is used:** In the early 1900s, women involved in the anti-suffrage movement **petitioned** the government in an attempt to rally support against the 19th Amendment.

# press conference



**What it is:** an event where the media receives new details from the government

**How it works:** Government officials host press conferences when they want the media to know about and report on specific information. By hosting a press conference, the government can control the narrative while also allowing the media to ask questions about the specific topic. Press conferences happen at all levels of government over different types of situations. Press conferences are important because they allow the press to hear from the government firsthand.

**How it is used:** The White House press secretary hosts **press conferences** frequently to inform the media, and therefore the public, about major issues the president is handling.

# prior restraint



**What it is:** government censorship that prohibits speech prior to it occurring

**How it works:** Prior restraint is a controversial action by the federal government that has often been struck down as unconstitutional. The government must justify its actions when using prior restraint, as the courts assume that any prior restraint is a violation of the 1st Amendment guarantee of freedom of speech. Examples of prior restraint are the government keeping a newspaper from publishing specific information, a court injunction to keep someone from talking about a certain topic, and a law requiring someone to have a permit before they can speak. Each prior restraint action is evaluated on a case-by-case basis to determine if it is constitutional or not.

**How it is used: Prior restraint** is permissible in situations where the government is attempting to protect national security, such as during times of war.

# probable cause



**What it is:** reasonable grounds for issuing a search or arrest warrant

**How it works:** To search someone's property, law enforcement agents must have a warrant. To obtain that warrant, they need probable cause that the individual they wish to search has committed an illegal activity. Probable cause can take many forms depending on the crime in question but can include fingerprint evidence, video footage, or the suspect being near the crime when it took place. A judge determines whether probable cause has been met before issuing a warrant, including arrest warrants. Probable cause is part of the 4th Amendment's protection from unreasonable searches and seizures.

**How it is used:** Before the government could arrest Billy, they needed **probable cause**, which they found through video footage of him near the scene of the crime.

# right to bear arms



**What it is:** the 2nd Amendment's core value of citizens being allowed to own guns

**How it works:** The 2nd Amendment states that citizens have the right to bear arms, which has been interpreted to mean that citizens are allowed to possess firearms for their own protection. There's controversy surrounding this interpretation though, since the amendment includes a statement about forming a militia. But the Supreme Court has interpreted the 2nd Amendment to mean that citizens are entitled to legally own firearms and that the government can't make laws that ban guns. The government can make laws about the process of purchasing a weapon as well as the appropriate uses and places to have a weapon.

**How it is used:** The **right to bear arms** is supported by many Americans, with 32 percent of adults personally owning a firearm, according to Pew Research.

# right to counsel



**What it is:** the fundamental right to have an attorney present during criminal trials

**How it works:** The 6th Amendment guarantees that every citizen has the right to counsel. Most Americans don't have extensive legal knowledge, so the prosecution (or the government) has an advantage during trial. The right to counsel is meant to ensure that the government can't take advantage of this knowledge gap. Originally applying only to the federal government, this right was incorporated into the states with the Supreme Court case *Gideon v. Wainwright* in 1963.

**How it is used:** To ensure that everyone has the **right to counsel**, the state and federal governments have an obligation to provide an attorney to all defendants, even if they can't afford one.

# scorekeeper



**What it is:** when the media tracks political campaigns and polling numbers

**How it works:** When the media acts as a scorekeeper, it spends time detailing the popularity of political candidates. To do this, it uses public opinion polls and approval ratings. By reporting on what percentage of people support candidates and their policies, and who's projected to win and lose, the media can influence public perception of a candidate and possibly the outcome of elections. Reporting the scores of politicians can also increase the competitiveness of an election.

**How it is used:** During the 2024 presidential election, many news outlets acted as **scorekeepers** when reporting on the polling data of the two candidates.

# scrutiny tests



*judicial review tests for equal protection cases*

**What it is:** examinations used by the courts to determine whether the government has violated the Equal Protection Clause of the 14th Amendment

**How it works:** When evaluating equal protection cases, courts use different tests. Strict scrutiny is the highest standard and requires the government to prove a compelling reason for violating fundamental rights, such as freedom of speech or the right to vote. For example, laws passed that ban the burning of the flag generally fail to pass the strict scrutiny test when challenged in court, as the state does not have a compelling interest in limiting this type of political speech. The intermediate scrutiny test is used primarily in cases of gender or sex discrimination and requires the government to prove that it has a significant interest in passing the law. For instance, a state law in Oklahoma allowing women to buy beer at age eighteen but men at twenty-one faced the intermediate scrutiny test when challenged in the courts. The rational basis test is used in cases where no fundamental rights are being violated. When the courts apply this test to laws being challenged, the government must prove it has a legitimate interest in creating the law. Generally, the court upholds these laws, unless they are seen as completely arbitrary.

**How it is used:** In 1955, the Supreme Court ruled that an Oklahoma law that prohibited non-licensed optometrists to fit lenses for eyeglasses passed the rational basis **scrutiny test** and was permissible.

# search and seizure

*investigating and arresting someone*

**What it is:** the government's ability to search people's property and take it, and them, into custody

**How it works:** Due to the 4th Amendment, the government must have probable cause to search and arrest someone. This protection keeps law enforcement agents accountable and helps to limit government power. Citizens can feel safe in their homes and not fear unlawful searches and seizures by the government. This right stems from the founding leaders' experiences during the American Revolution when Great Britain issued writs of assistance, allowing government officials to search anyone for any reason.

**How it is used:** While people are protected from unwarranted **searches and seizures** in their homes, their cars can be searched without a warrant because there is a lower expectation of privacy with vehicles compared to houses.

# search warrant

*legal authorization to search someone*

**What it is:** a document needed to lawfully search someone and their property

**How it works:** In most cases, if the government wants to search someone, they must obtain a warrant. To get a warrant, law enforcement must have probable cause. If they meet this threshold, a judge will issue a warrant specific to the place to be searched. Search warrants must be executed by government officials, such as law enforcement agents. The necessity of having search warrants limits the government's power and protects the rights of citizens.

**How it is used:** There are many rules for the execution of a **search warrant**, including that officers can't search places or individuals not explicitly listed on the warrant itself.

# selective incorporation

*applying the Bill of Rights to the states*

**What it is:** the case-by-case process of incorporating the rights and freedoms in the Bill of Rights into state governments

**How it works:** When the Bill of Rights was first put into effect, it limited only the federal government. Many states had their own bills of rights, but they were different from the federal government's. Over time, citizens challenged the laws of their states for violating the Bill of Rights. When the courts ruled on these cases in favor of the citizen, the federal right was incorporated at the state level. This has happened over time on a selective basis. As a result, the states can't violate many of the rights and freedoms listed in the Bill of Rights, but there are still some elements that haven't been incorporated.

**How it is used:** The 1925 Supreme Court case *Gitlow v. New York* kick-started **selective incorporation** when the court ruled that a New York law violated the 1st Amendment's protection of freedom of speech.

# self-incrimination



**What it is:** the act of someone saying information that can lead to their own arrest or conviction

**How it works:** The 5th Amendment protects citizens from having to testify against themselves. This protection from self-incrimination allows individuals to remain silent when being interrogated by law enforcement. It also means that criminal defendants don't need to take the witness stand in their trials if they believe that something they say could lead the jury to believe they committed the crime in question. When someone is arrested, they're read the Miranda warnings, which include the right to remain silent. In cases where people aren't read these rights and don't know their protections against self-incrimination, the case can be dismissed.

**How it is used:** The protection against **self-incrimination** comes from the 1966 Supreme Court case *Miranda v. Arizona*, when Miranda confessed without knowing his 5th Amendment right to remain silent.

# slander



**What it is:** speaking untrue statements about someone with malicious intent

**How it works:** Slander, also called defamation, isn't protected by the 1st Amendment. If someone commits slander, they have knowingly spoken falsehoods about another person with the intention of damaging their reputation. Slander, similar to libel (also defined in this chapter), is difficult to prove. In cases of slander against a public figure, there must be proof that the person knew their words were false and that they had malicious intent. Only statements of fact, not opinions, are considered.

**How it is used:** To win a **slander** claim, the victim must prove that they suffered actual harm from the slanderous statement and that it was shared with another person.

# symbolic speech



**What it is:** a type of speech that's expressive in nature

**How it works:** Symbolic speech, or speech through expression, is protected under the 1st Amendment. It's not always verbal in nature and can include things like artwork, music, clothing, and actions such as burning the flag or protesting. This type of speech is protected when the message it conveys is understandable to the public, but it can't cause physical harm or property damage.

**How it is used:** The Supreme Court case *Texas v. Johnson* ruled that burning the American flag is protected as a form of both **symbolic speech** and political speech.

# true threats



**What it is:** statements that make others fear that they'll be harmed

**How it works:** True threats aren't protected under the 1st Amendment. True threats are statements of intention to cause harm to another person. To be classified as a true threat, the statement must convey a serious intent to cause bodily harm or death to another and instill fear in that individual. This speech doesn't need to result in harm being carried out, but if the speaker intends to communicate a threat, it's classified as unprotected speech.

**How it is used:** An example of a **true threat** is someone threatening to kill another person over social media.

# watchdog



**What it is:** the role of the media to keep an eye on government activity and report to the people when wrongdoing occurs

**How it works:** The media has many roles in the American government. Perhaps its most important is that of a watchdog, where it investigates the actions of people in positions of power and reports to the people. The people need the media to fulfill this role so they can make informed decisions and participate effectively in the political process. This role places responsibility on the media to inform people when the government overreaches. Additionally, it helps with transparency and accountability with the government, as the government knows the media acts in this capacity.

**How it is used:** In 1971, *The New York Times* and *The Washington Post* acted as **watchdogs** when they published leaked government documents known as the Pentagon Papers, which showed how the government had misled the American people regarding the Vietnam War.

# Index

Linkage institutions, 150

Lobbying, grassroots, 146

Lobbyists, 151. *See also* Interest groups;
	Revolving door politics

Logrolling, 57

Majority leader, 57

Majority rule with minority rights, 33

Mandatory spending, 58

Media. *See* Civil liberties and the media

Merit-based system, 96

Midterm elections, 151

Minority leader, 58–59

Misdemeanors, 121

Monetary policy, 59

Narrowcasting, 187–88

National conventions, 152

National debt, 97

National Security Council, 97

National Voter Registration Act, 152–53

Naturalization, 98

Natural rights, 17

Necessary and Proper Clause, 59–60

New Federalism, 34

Nullification, 34–35

Obscene speech, 188

Oligarchy, 17

Omnibus bill, 60

Open primary, 153

Orders, executive, 89

Original jurisdiction, 121–22

Override, power of, 60

Oversight, congressional, 49

Parliamentary system, 18

Parole, 122

Participatory democracy, 35

Party identification, 153

Patronage, political, 99

Per curiam opinions, 122–23

Petitioners, 123

Petitions, to the government, 188

Plaintiffs, 123

Plea bargains, 124

Pluralist democracy, 35–36

Pocket veto, 98

Police powers, 36

Policy gridlock, 61

Political action committees (PACs), 154. *See
	also* Super PACs

Political efficacy, 154

Political ideology, 155

Political participation. *See also specific terms*
	about: overview of, 133
	related terms and definitions, 134–72

Political parties, 155. *See also specific parties*

Political patronage, 99

Political polarization, 156

Political socialization, 156

Politico model, 61–62

Politics, defined, 18

Polling locations, 157

Polls, public opinion, 142, 147, 159, 191

Poll tax, 157

Popular sovereignty, 36–37

Pork barrel legislation, 62

Powers. *See* Constitution

Preamble (Constitution), 37

Precincts, 158

Preponderance of evidence, 124

Presidential Succession Act, 100

President of the Senate, 62–63

President of the United States, 73, 99. *See also*
	Executive branch

Speech, freedom of, 183. *See also* Censorship;
    Compelled speech; Hate speech; Imminent
    lawless action test; Libel; Obscene speech;
    Prior restraint; Slander; Symbolic speech

Spending. *See* Finance

Split-ticket voting, 164

Spouse, First, 90

Staff, chief of, 78

Standing committees, 70

State, chief of, 79. *See also* Executive branch;
    President of the United States

State, U.S. Department of, 86

State of the Union Address, 102

States

    20th Amendment and, 22

    concurrent powers and, 26

    cooperative federalism and, 27

    dual federalism and, 28

    extradition and, 30

    nullification and, 34–35

    police powers and, 36

    reserved powers, 38–39

    Supremacy Clause and, 41

Statutory law, 128

Straight-ticket voting, 165

Strict constructionists, 128

Subpoenas, 129

Suffrage, 165. *See also* 19th Amendment

Superdelegates, 166

Super PACs, 166

Super Tuesday, 167

Supremacy Clause, 41

Supreme Court. *See also* Judicial branch

Swing states, 167

Symbolic speech, 195

Tariffs, 103

Taxes. *See* Finance

Think tanks, 168

Third parties, 168

Threats, true, 196

Top-two primary, 169

Transportation, U.S. Department of, 86–87

Treason, 130

Treasury, U.S. Department of, 87

Trial by jury, 131

True threats, 196

Trustee model, 70–71

Two-party system, 169

Unitary system, 20

United States government, this book and, 6–7.
    *See also specific branches and topics*

U.S. courts. *See* Judicial branch

Veteran Affairs, U.S. Department of, 87–88

Vetoes, 60, 78, 96, 98, 161

Veto power, 103

Vice president, 104

Voter apathy, 170

Voter registration, 170

Voter turnout, 171

Voting Rights Act, 171

Voting rights and activities (political
    participation). *See also specific terms*

    about: overview of, 133

    related terms and definitions, 134–72

War Powers Act, 104

Watchdog, media as, 196

Ways and Means Committee, 71

Whips, 71–72

White House press corps, 105

Winner-take-all system, 172

Writs of certiorari, 132

# About the Author

**Emily Lewellen** was born and raised in Northern California. She earned a BS in education in history and an MA in history from Northern Arizona University. She has more than a decade of experience teaching United States history, United States government, AP government and politics, and AP United States history. In 2021, Emily was named Indiana's History Teacher of the Year by The Gilder Lehrman Institute of American History. She lives with her family in Indiana.